LOOKING AT LONDON

Illustrated walks through a changing city

ARTHUR KUTCHER

Introduction by Wayland Kennet

with 90 drawings and a map

THAMES AND HUDSON

Acknowledgments

This book has drawn much information and insight from *The Buildings of England, London*, I and II, by Sir Nikolaus Pevsner, and from *Victorian London* by Priscilla Metcalf. Other books which have provided useful reference material are *Landlords to London* by Simon Jenkins, *Changing Ideals in Modern Architecture* by Peter Collins, *London: Metropolis and Region* by John M. Hall, *The City of London Churches* by John Betjeman, *The City of London, Its Architectural Heritage* by David Crawford, *Goodbye London* by Christopher Booker and Candida Lycett Green, *Hawksmoor* by Kerry Downes, and *Wren* by Margaret Whinney.

164243

Library of Congress Catalog card number 78–53473

Filmset in Great Britain by Keyspools Ltd, Golborne, Lancashire
Printed and bound in Great Britain by Unwin Brothers Ltd, Old Woking, Surrey

Contents

Introduction

FIVE YEARS AGO Arthur Kutcher wrote and illustrated a book called *The New Jerusalem*, which was one of the main ways the world found out about the dreadful eyesores being built and being planned for the ruin of that small, lovely, and already enough tormented old city. The world reacted, and some of the eyesores were not built after all.

This book which deals with the equally small and, once you look at it, equally interesting old city of central London, ought to have the same effect. It is now twenty years since Harold Macmillan, then Prime Minister, personally took two decisions which led in due course to London's becoming the most vandalized of all the Western European capitals. He overrode all official recommendations and permitted both the demolition of the Euston Propylaeum, and the construction of the Hilton Hotel in Park Lane.

The first of these two idiotic gestures towards 'modernization' marked, happily, the beginning of better times for preservation as such. It raised such an outcry, culminating in the Smithson's incandescent book of 1968, that never again was a single building of such importance allowed to be destroyed, and it became possible for Parliament to pass the two cornerstones of our present conservation law, the Civic Amenities Act of 1967 and the Part IV of the Town and Country Planning Act of 1968. The second act of vandalism, the permitting of the Hilton Hotel, conversely and tragically ushered in the age of high building in London, which obsesses this book. Mr Kutcher's remorselessly right drawings and his beguilingly venomous perambulations show with dreadful clarity that all we can now hope for in central London is a desperate last stand to save one or two remaining civilized scenes and vistas. (Outside the centre, things are not so bad.) That Kutcher's last stand should be made is all the more important since London was, after all, a beautiful city; it used to be midway between the villages of Amsterdam and Dublin in more senses than one. It is, of course, too late – too late by twenty years, since the Victorian height restriction of 80–100 feet was scrapped by Macmillan – to hope that London can ever again match Paris or Rome or Copenhagen or Stockholm. London is now halfway between those cities and the others: Frankfurt and Düsseldorf which were bombed out of existence, Cleveland and Toronto which were never of human scale in the first place.

But what can be saved, must be. The old subsidy on high-rise housing has long since gone; in Liverpool the 'high-rise housing' of 1960 is already coming down. Planning permissions are now limited to four years; if you haven't used your permission in that time you have to apply again. This provision, if boldly applied, would make it impossible for a new Seifert ever to arise. Seifert achieved his amazing predominance as the destroyer of our once pleasing capital by the trick of sitting on planning permissions granted in the un-townscape-conscious forties and fifties and then, after the Macmillan relaxation, forcing through applications for 'less bulky' and 'more civilized' designs which *bien entendu* would be four times as high, under threat of going back and using the original permissions.

But still the high buildings crowd forward. This book gives the appalling figure: since 1965 when the GLC was given power to approve or reject buildings more than 125 feet high (150 feet in some places) they have approved no less than 2,089 applications. This of course is equivalent to a general blanket approval, and the mere existence of the machinery of administration wastes human resources.

London now stands poised, after a five-year check because of the most welcome collapse of the property market in 1973 (not the only good result of the 1973 Arab-Israeli war, but much the best), for a new building boom as North Sea oil is exploited for the benefit of our national economy. It must be the first duty of all planners, councillors, architects and ministers responsible for this city to see that never again are the atrocities, chronicled here with such restraint and such historical polish, allowed to resume. The final destruction of Wren's City by Holford and Seifert has never been better analyzed, and the description of Gibberd's 'Arundel Great Court', which destroys the last vestige of proportionableness remaining around St Clement Danes and St Mary-le-Strand, ought to become famous. So, on the positive side, ought Mr Kutcher's account of the saving of Trafalgar Square; a story which ended, for once, in good will and good humour all round.

This book does not recommend a social or administrative solution: it breathes the spirit of Jane Jacobs and Pevsner. The dilemma remains. If Paris is still, with one exception so horrifying as to burn the lesson into all eyes for ever, a low city, that is because France is and always has been a country of strong central powers. The same goes for Rome. Perhaps we could learn from Copenhagen; who knows? But much the best outcome would be if we in our generation, as has happened in many generations before us, were democratically to learn from our mistakes; if we in our millions were to rise up and demand from those we elect to have power over us that they put away all corruption whether public or private, that they put away the sloppy belief that if you can't measure something in money it doesn't exist, and that they now in 1978 and here in central London begin adamantly to defend the human scale, the natural street forms, the careful design and craft, and the interesting skylines which our parents have left us, against the 'nameless dread' which speculative and big commercial developers inspire. The signs are not good; the Department of the Environment's corps of investigators has been reduced. The Office Development control is being run down. Ministerial statements implying excessive preservationist rigour in the past are not lacking, and you will read them further on.

There is no need to demand the preservation of everything: it is mainly our forlorn experience of the replacement that makes us shudder at demolition. Contemporary architects have been known to build well: very well. As well as ever. If they have done it outside the central London of this book, the fault is that of a system which dares not treat our national capital as a national, i.e. central Government, responsibility.

WAYLAND KENNET

London's Character

FAMOUS DESCRIPTIONS OF LONDON, mirroring its changing character, have been as varied and contradictory as the great city itself. For the sixteenth-century Scottish poet William Dunbar London was the

> Flower of cities all
> Gem of all joy, Jasper of jocunditie.

The diarist John Evelyn recorded a less poetic aspect of the expanding city when he reported in 1661 that 'the air . . . is here eclipsed with such a cloud of sulphor, as the sun itself is hardly able to penetrate . . . and the weary traveller at many miles distance, sooner smells, than sees the city to which he repairs.'

In the eighteenth century, Dr Samuel Johnson pointed out that 'If you wish to have a just notion of the magnitude of this city, you must not be satisfied with seeing its great streets and squares, but must survey the innumerable little lanes and courts. It is not in the showy evolutions of buildings, but in the multiplicity of human habitations which are crowded together, that the wonderful immensity of London consists.' Surveying a London even more immense than Dr Johnson's, a German guidebook writer, A. W. Grube, was inspired to remark in 1868 that 'The prospect of this city fills one with the shudder felt when confronting the sea. The magic of London lies in its inexhaustible extent.'

The clouds of sulphur dioxide which greeted John Evelyn, and which prompted Shelley to remark that 'Hell is a city much like London – a populous and smoky city', were finally banished by the Clean Air Act of 1956. Dr Johnson's little lanes and courts have long since ceased to be innumerable and have become treasured rarities from which planners and speculators still take occasional bites. Victorian London's sense of immeasurable extent was the result not merely of its physical size, but of the seemingly endless succession of its intimate and meandering streets, few of which permitted vistas of any great length, and of the relative modesty and irregular placement of London's monumental buildings, which refrained from providing the predictable procession of massive landmarks which make distance easily measurable in continental cities. The astounding impression of the vastness of Victorian London survived in expanded form until about a decade ago, when the wave of high-rise construction which made London the European city richest in this form of building also shrank the apparent size of the metropolis and converted Herr Grube's perception into a memory.

The vast extent of the metropolis, built up in a finely-sifted combination of order and variety, subdivided into areas of strong local flavour and punctuated by great parks, squares, and public gardens, has a multiplicity of historic origins. While other medieval cities focused on a single centre, London was and remains what Lewis Mumford called 'a confederation of historic communities'. The absence of foreign military threat and the relative weakness of central political authority were reflected by the numerous sub-centres of medieval growth dispersed around the polar arrangement of the royal/monastic complex at Westminster and the merchants' redoubt in the City, at either end of the sweeping bend in the Thames. The lack of absolutist power also meant that repeated royal decrees prohibiting further expansion had no effect. The first of many was Elizabeth I's edict of 1580 establishing a three-mile-wide green belt around old London. It was simply ignored by the developers. With royal authority powerless to control encroachments on rural land and the erosion of rural vistas, private citizens raised furious protests and in one case the lawyers of Gray's Inn assaulted the builders.

Both the suburbanization of medieval London and the generally futile attempts to halt it grew out of the English attachment to the countryside. To accommodate the city-dweller's taste for suburban living and to allow an escape from the crowded, polluted, and disease-ridden City of London, the techniques of speculative property development took on a degree of sophistication unknown elsewhere, producing the estates, the leasehold system, and the London square. The first of them in the West End, St James's Square, was begun just before the Plague of 1665 and the Great Fire of 1666 added impetus to the flight from the City. The spreading waves of seventeenth- and eighteenth-century development had been made possible by the Dissolution of the Monasteries which followed Henry VIII's break with the papacy in 1538. The Crown seized the extensive monastic and ecclesiastical holdings in the belt of rural land around the old city and granted or sold them to favoured members of the nobility, while the vast unbuildable marshlands north-west of the Royal Palace at Whitehall became the nucleus of the Royal Parks.

Visitors may be puzzled by London's variety of building materials and heights, bewildered by its profusion of architectural styles, and confused by its apparently perverse street layout. Londoners are immensely proud of their city's traditional close-grained variety and manifest visual inconsistency, and some may even confess that however much they admire the carefully orchestrated logic of Haussmann's Paris, it bores them. Despite this, Londoners feel a strong attachment to the harmonious proportions and consistency of the city's classical architecture, Palladian, Georgian and Regency. Those who lack this kind of broadly inclusive and indeed contradictory taste are condemned to repeat the misfortune of the nineteenth-century 'battlers of the styles' whose ideologies compelled them to ignore one half of London or the other.

Nowhere outside Italy has architecture been the subject of more acrimonious public debate than in England. The 'Battle of the Styles' usually refers to the Victorian dispute between classicists and Gothicists, but the term could be equally well applied to a whole series of architectural skirmishes which began with the introduction of the Italian Renaissance style in the seventeenth century. The Palladians, who were often more convincing as pamphleteers than as designers, savaged the Baroque works of Christopher Wren and Nicholas Hawksmoor; the classicist eclectics of the later eighteenth century led by Robert Adam hammered the Palladians; the neo-classical stucco of John Nash was reviled as soundly by his contemporaries as were the neo-Gothic works of George Gilbert Scott and George Edmund Street by their technologically infatuated adversaries. In our own time the clashes have taken on a new bitterness: the modernists' mechanized brigades first overran the Banker's classicist rearguard and were well on their way to grinding the whole of traditional Western architecture to dust when they were finally brought to a halt by the stout resistance of the Man in the Street.

The styles which provoked such fierce controversy were nearly all imported from abroad. France and Italy alternated as the main sources of inspiration, with considerable reference made in the later nineteenth century to the architecture of Holland, Flanders, and northern Germany. The true achievement of English architects, modernists excepted, lay in their ingenious adaptation of continental styles to London's social and historic pattern, and in the adjustments they contrived to suit local qualities of light and climate. London's characteristic mixture of Renaissance and Baroque Portland stone, dark Georgian brickwork, glowing neo-classic stucco, sombre Gothic polychromy, and red-brick, banded stone and terracotta all meeting the sky in a combination of cornices, balustrades, and pinnacled

The core of London's historic townscape was the City of London with its intricate medieval street pattern, above which rose Christopher Wren's delicate Gothic and Baroque church spires, crowned by St Paul's dome. The high-rise construction of the last decade has introduced a new kind of dominance

gables, is as striking for its overall harmony as for its rich variety. Regardless of the stylistic disputes which inspired such diversity, the choice of materials and refinement of detail, responding to the varying but often shadowless London light, and to sinuous streets and terminated vistas, show a strong sense of townscape continuity. London's historically evolved, finely-scaled graphic pattern of black, white and red serves as an unforgettable reminder that the eighteenth- and nineteenth-century battles of the styles, for all their verbal acrimony, were the disputes of civilized, visually sensitive designers.

In the case of more formal townscape compositions the adaptation of foreign styles to local circumstances became the springboard to a creativity which produced unique urban forms. A generation after Inigo Jones introduced the paved Renaissance piazza at Covent Garden, it had been transformed at St James and in Bloomsbury into the green London square. John Nash bent the rigid axiality of continental neo-classicism into graceful curves which pleased the English sense for the picturesque, and later Victorian neo-classic and neo-Gothic designers produced skyline compositions which substituted complex individuality and subtle interaction for the monolithic stasis of the late neo-classic townscape prevalent on the Continent.

In reviewing the major stages in the evolution of London's urban character it is important to remember that the forms and details of traditional designs were conceived urbanistically, and that every major architectural style had a corresponding townscape layout appropriate to it: Georgian terraces were ideally grouped around squares, the characteristic colonnades of neo-classicism heightened the effect of axial layouts, with the porticos terminating vistas, while the textured relief and variegated skylines of Victorian designs were intended to create the perspective effects of 'street architecture'.

Thomas Archer's St John's, Smith Square, is a highly original Anglican Baroque work, centrally planned on a cross-axis with four towers at the corners. The church's Portland stone contrasted with the contemporary red-brick houses which surrounded it. Some Queen Anne houses still introduce St John's north portico.

Unprotected view (see pages 123–24)

Medieval, Renaissance and Baroque

Before the seventeenth century the townscape vernacular had been characterized by a process of growth which clung tightly to pragmatic Saxon street lines, rolling with the topography, skirting the marshlands and following the ecologically dictated boundaries of ancient farmsteads. The centres of development in medieval London were focused at Westminster Abbey and in the City, where ordinary buildings of half-timber construction faced the street on narrow plots, often with gardens behind. Larger groupings like the Temple, later Inns of Court, and the Royal Palace were laid out along collegiate lines with linked courtyards of various proportions enclosed by seemingly random collections of structures of various heights, sizes and materials.

The revolution, begun in 1631 by Inigo Jones with London's first Renaissance square at Covent Garden, was expanded upon by Christopher Wren, whose rejected Baroque scheme for rebuilding the post-Fire City was a multi-centred axial network which conformed to the latest developments in Parisian townplanning. Wren's works, like those of his pupil Nicholas Hawksmoor, were conceived urbanistically, and used the Renaissance science of perspective as an aid to design. Wren's intent was to please the intellect by striking the chords of visual harmony based on what he called the natural beauty of geometric proportion. The impact of Hawksmoor's use of geometry is quite different; the powerful forms of his designs evoke a direct emotional response and the contrast between his works and those of Wren points to the eighteenth-century theorists' distinction between the Beautiful and the Sublime, the former arising from the perception of harmonious proportion, the latter from the confrontation with the vast and awe-inspiring creations of turbulent nature.

In medieval times the principal approach to Westminster Abbey and the Sanctuary had been from Tothill Street, through a great gate. Wren's scheme for Whitehall and the Abbey would have framed the view to the west front in a monumental archway. His pupil Hawksmoor added twin towers to the west front in the eighteenth century, and the recent demolition of a Victorian corner block opened this view from Tothill Street

Despite their obvious preference for the up-to-date styles of Italy and France, Wren and Hawksmoor retained respect for the old Gothic styles and designed well in them when called upon. Wren proposed the completion of the west towers of Westminster Abbey 'in the Gothic Form' and warned that 'to deviate from the old Form would be to run into a Disagreeable Mixture which no Person of good Taste could relish.' Hawksmoor followed Wren's advice in his Gothic design for the Abbey's west towers. He also demonstrated a sense of place in the modest brick arcade at Stable Yard, which blends quietly with its sixteenth-century neighbours at St James's Palace. Given full rein his expressive talent could result in awesome works; his 220-foot high steeple at Christ Church, Spitalfields, is a truly hair-raising example. Hawksmoor's unforgettable landmark was denounced by a Palladian detractor as 'the most preposterous pile in Europe'.

Palladian London and the Golden Age

The Palladian style, like the Anglican Baroque, employed features of Roman classical architecture revived and transformed by the Italian Renaissance, but while Baroque architects took pride in the originality and expressive power of their designs, the Palladian circle which gathered around the enthusiastic architectural amateur Lord Burlington in the 1720s insisted on strict adherence to the classical principles brought to England a century before by Inigo Jones and derived in turn from the works and writings of the Italian Renaissance architect Palladio, whose *Four Books of Architecture* echoed the rules of building formulated by Vitruvius in the second century. The English Palladians mercilessly derided the works of their Baroque predecessors and quickly spread their style by means of publications. The Palladians' emphasis on rationalist clarity and rote-learning made their principles particularly well suited as a guide to good taste for the newly-risen politicians of the reformist Whig party, and for the builders whose large-scale residential schemes were beginning to spread across the fields of the West End. The rare Palladian mansions which survived a wave of redevelopment in the 1920s show the carefully polished restraint of rule-book architecture. The greatest exponent of the style was James Gibbs, whose church designs rise above the rancour of his colleagues and show a community of spirit with his Baroque predecessors.

The aesthetic philosophy of the eighteenth-century classicists was derived from the cosmology of pagan antiquity. The mathematical harmonies

Some of the finest examples of the English domestic Baroque style are found in Queen Anne's Gate. The houses are particularly noteworthy for their elaborately carved hooded door-cases. Above the intimate street and its delicate buildings rise the thundering forms of the new Home Office on the site of the Victorian Queen Anne's Mansions

underlying architecture, music, and rhetoric were tied to the principles of astronomy and the proportions of the human body. The fine arts never progressed; following nature their changes were cyclical. It was thus possible for the Georgian age to appreciate works of classical harmony not as relics of a bygone era but as fresh, contemporary creations. For eighteenth-century theorists 'taste' meant a cultivated recognition of the objective beauty of the orders and proportions of antiquity.

Classical artists and writers seem to have had no interest in self-revelation and self-glorification; their goal was to please, amuse, and instruct their audiences. By mid-century a subtle change with far-reaching implications arrived with the archaeological researches of James Stuart at Athens and Robert Adam at Diocletian's palace at Spalato. The unquestioned supremacy of the old Vitruvian/Palladian classicism was challenged and ultimately replaced by the newly-discovered lucidity of ancient Greece and the decorative refinement of second-century Rome. When Robert Adam wrote that 'Nothing is more sterile and disgustful than to see for ever the dull repetition of Dorick, Ionick and Corinthian entablatures in their usual proportions', he introduced a conception of 'taste' in line with the modern idea – the expression of individual whim irreducible to a formula. When later eighteenth-century theorists, expanding on the concept of the Sublime, advanced the notion of 'a certain disorder' as the prime aesthetic merit, and when landscape gardeners strove to achieve 'pleasing confusion' in their designs, the groundwork was laid for the nineteenth-century Picturesque and for the 'pleasing gloom' of later Victorian architecture.

Palladian London is familiar from Hogarth's etchings, and though the image he presents of the horrors of Gin Lane set against a picture of foppish dilettantes, unwashed and heavily perfumed, lounging about their coffee houses, has an element of caricature, the stark contrasts of mid-eighteenth-century London cannot be denied. Radiant private splendour co-existed with staggering public squalor; the urbane mansions of the *cognoscenti*, with façades displaying exquisite classical scholarship, faced each other across the mire of unpaved streets.

Classicism at Green Park: Spencer House, centre, is a design of the Golden Age, but a distinctly non-Palladian composition with a sense of elemental power rather than correctness and delicacy. The engaged portico, ignoring Vitruvius, is proportioned like an archaic Greek temple. Next to it on the right is Charles Barry's early Victorian Bridgewater House, much larger but showing gentlemanly refinement combined with inventive detail. Both are works of classicism with an individual flavour

Victoria Square is a late neo-classical square built in 1838 in the style of Nash's stuccoed West Strand Improvements. Its pleasant sense of enclosure fell victim to its large modern neighbour

The most significant achievement of the Palladian style in London occurred when its proportions, based on the repeated rhythms of the double square and the Golden Section, were applied to the vernacular brick architecture of the London terrace house. The red-brick domestic style of the later seventeenth century with high roofs and timber eaves had been 'classicized' by post-Great Fire regulations which replaced the eaves with brick parapets and cornices. Builders' architecture was further transformed when the fire regulations of 1709 banned heavy timber sashes flush with the façade and decreed slender frames set well back in the brickwork, exposing stuccoed soffits. 'Burlington's Harry' Flitcroft subjected this arrangement to the proportional rigour of the Palladian formulae at mid-century, and when the combination of pragmatic vernacular texture and classical refinement was codified in the building regulations of 1774, the result was the Golden Age of Georgian architecture, which coincided with the great surge in estate building and moulded the character of much of central London.

The estates were large-scale residential developments laid out in a patchwork of unrelated grids adjusted to the old linear settlements like the villages of St Martin's, St Giles, and St Marylebone. The grids often met, or rather collided at the boundaries of former ecclesiastical manors, and at rural lanes. The landed aristocrats who built up the fields acquired by their forebears after the Dissolution had neither the desire nor the power to link their estates in larger townscape compositions. By leasing building plots rather than selling them, they 'farmed' their lands, 'the best crop being bricks and mortar'. Their rural preferences were also shown by the siting of their London mansions, usually placed on the north sides of squares with principal rooms having vistas away from the city and towards the wooded hills of Hampstead and Highgate. The layout of the estates also reflected the Georgian social hierarchy with a graduated system of humble mews, modest streets, and larger avenues culminating in grand houses facing the squares which were the core of development and remain the most distinctive feature of the eighteenth-century townscape. The squares developed in the late seventeenth and early eighteenth centuries were bounded by houses put up by individual leaseholders; those of the Golden Age were enclosed by speculatively conceived and uniformly designed terraces. Of the twenty-one squares laid out in central London between the seventeenth and early nineteenth centuries, only Bedford Square in Bloomsbury has survived with its original buildings intact, preserving the unique Georgian mixture of large-scale uniformity and small-scale refinement of detail.

Neo-classical compositions often sacrificed traditional church orientation for visual effect. St Marylebone faces north to close the vista framed by Nash's twin Grecian terraces in York Gate, south of Regent's Park.
Unprotected view

Neo-classic London

The flowering of the neo-classic style in London coincided with the regency of the Prince of Wales, later George IV. While Palladianism was a version of Vitruvian classicism three times removed from its Roman source, neo-classicism was the first revival to draw its forms from direct archaeological investigation of the ruins of ancient Greece, though it used details from fifth-century Athens in very un-Greek large-scale axial compositions. It was also the last unified international style before Victorian architecture broke up into a welter of co-existing and seemingly contradictory revivals. Neo-classical designers displayed an extraordinary passion for unity. While previous styles had existed in pairs – Anglican Baroque and Queen Anne, Palladian and Georgian – the one in Portland stone for grand display, the other in brick for domestic purposes, in neo-classic compositions palaces, banks, hospitals, government offices, shops and ordinary houses were all subsumed behind stucco façades and Grecian colonnades.

Neo-classic townscape was characterized by simplicity and clarity, with broad avenues lined with uniform buildings focusing vistas toward axially aligned monuments. Designers were particularly fascinated by the phenomenon of parallax produced by the procession of long colonnades. Baroque compositions of the previous century resembled those of neo-classicism in their ambitious scale, but where Baroque schemes emphasized rhythmic vitality and multiple diversions, neo-classic designers disposed prismatic forms along relentless single axes, and where the Baroque was rich, sensuous, and colourful, neo-classicism was strict, spare and intellectually precise.

The style, also known as 'Regency' or as 'Romantic classicism', idealized nature and classical antiquity as each receded in time or space from the nineteenth-century urban world. The chaste uniformity of neo-classicism's characteristic Ionic colonnades suited the taste of a still careful and rather parsimonious commercial and professional class, while the extravagant scale and inherent theatricality of neo-classic townscape compositions made them a favourite vehicle for expressing despotic visions of grandeur.

In London there had been a relative dearth of monumental architecture on a continental scale until the advent of the style. For political as well as aesthetic reasons the capital had not been considered the appropriate site for awe-inspiring architectural display. The genuinely astounding works created for the aristocracy who owned much of London were reserved for the quiet English countryside. The architectural tone within the city was set by

more pragmatic works motivated by a dry commercial sense, like the sound, unflamboyant development of the estates. Continental neo-classic grandeur, monitored by a careful regard for rentability, and modified by a strong sense for the picturesque, was introduced to London in 1812 by a country house architect, John Nash, who maintained close ties with the Prince Regent. His design of the Regent's Park scheme brought the impressive scale of rural aristocratic compositions to the city, merging the concept of the palatial country residence with that of the London terrace house to meet a growing market for mass middle-class housing in a bucolic setting.

The dramatic transformation of London's townscape wrought by Nash's neo-classic stucco was the subject of an ironic verse of 1826:

> Augustus at Rome was for building renown'd,
> And of marble he left what of brick he had found;
> But is not our Nash, too, a very great master? –
> He finds us all brick and leaves us all plaster.

The reaction to Nash's colonnaded neo-classicism set in soon enough; Italian Renaissance palazzi, 'astylar', that is without columns, appeared throughout London with their heavy cornices, pedimented windows and corner quoins, following the style's introduction in the 1830s by Charles Barry in Pall Mall. The use of stucco gradually receded but it continued to be consistently employed by architects and builders who used to advantage the terminated vistas offered by unmatched eighteenth-century street grids. By stucco-fronting houses which closed the view they provided the 'black and white' contrasts typical of the cumulative eighteenth- and nineteenth-century townscapes with dark Georgian brick façades framing neo-classic stucco.

The lost thread of Victorian and Edwardian townscape
The building of Victorian London forms the counterpart to the achievements of the Georgian and neo-classic eras. At their most characteristic, Georgian and Regency builders had laid out large tracts on virgin land or, in the case of

the swath of Nash's Regent Street, redeveloped 'comprehensively' according to quite explicit urbanistic guidelines; the Victorian redevelopment of large parts of central London followed the individual judgment and fantasy of architects and their clients. Although parts of the West End estates were rebuilt when the original leases ran out in the later nineteenth century, the bulk of Victorian construction took place in the interstices between the estate grids, along the old commercial thoroughfares and some new ones, and in the City of London. Victorian rebuilders have often been condemned for the extensive destruction they wrought, and for the insensitivity of their replacements. Although the criticism was merited in some cases, in others Victorian architects retained older buildings, humbly completing or augmenting them in the original style. Very often they merely refronted buildings of the seventeenth and eighteenth centuries to bring them in line with their concept of 'street architecture', while keeping the original interiors intact. The 'gutting' of historic buildings is a concept the Victorians would find difficult to understand. When demolition took place, it was often only partial; usually parts of the old structure and fitments were intelligently reused. Victorian architects were also fond of referring in their compositions and details to historic features of the locality, and to the architectural devices of their older neighbours, with townscape themes being repeated and elaborated by successive generations of builders. Designs were further localized by the development of 'area styles', identified by the districts where they were most prevalent. Late neo-classic stucco palazzi in long terraces were 'Kensington Italianate' (to use Osbert Lancaster's expressive terminology), 'Pont Street Dutch' displayed Hanseatic red brick and big gables, the 'Mayfair style' was French Renaissance and Jacobethan in red brick and terracotta, and the 'Charing Cross style' was noted for its large and freely eclectic hotels in Second Empire Portland and Bath stone. The City of London had its own characteristic 'Bankers' classic' and Baroque as well as the Venetian Gothic and Italio-Byzantine styles preferred by smaller firms, particularly by those engaged in foreign trade.

The Victorian/Edwardian skyline of Whitehall is seen here from Carlton House Terrace, a crowning work of the Regency. This view presents the result of the nineteenth-century 'Battle of the Styles': the early Victorian Gothic Revival Houses of Parliament, the High Victorian neo-Renaissance Foreign Office, Norman Shaw's red-brick eclectic New Scotland Yard and, in the foreground, the late Victorian/Edwardian Baroque domes of the Admiralty. On the far right are Hawksmoor's Westminster Abbey towers, and left of them, peering uncomprehendingly at it all, is the Millbank Tower, 1963. Unprotected view

The changes in London's urban fabric at macro-scale were wrought by the Olympian works of Victorian engineering which brought mass transport, sanitation and the beginnings of unified government to the metropolis. The London and Birmingham Railway's Euston Station, designed by Philip Hardwick in the Italian style and opened in 1838 was the first of the rail termini which were to ring the central area with their monumental forms. The impact of Euston's construction upon the area adjacent was compared by Charles Dickens with 'the first shock of a great earthquake leaving in its wake unnatural hills and accidental ponds'. Euston was pulled down in 1962 as part of British Rail's spasmodic modernization programme. Other stations, most notably Paddington, St Pancras, King's Cross, and Liverpool Street, their sheds vaulted with sweeping cast-iron arches, still face the city with classical or Gothic façades of distinction. London's placid riverscape changed dramatically as great cast-iron road and rail bridges spanned the Thames on massive pillars, while the river's increasing pollution and a series of cholera epidemics at mid-century led to the creation of London's first unified administrative body, the Metropolitan Board of Works. The forerunner of the present Greater London Council was set up in 1855 with the primary responsibility of laying plans for a metropolitan sewer system, which was completed along with the stately granite-faced Thames Embankment in the late 1860s.

Plans to relieve the swelling traffic inching its way along the by now tortured web of old streets in the heart of the city led to a series of new links connecting main thoroughfares in a more or less rational pattern. A few of the new projects, like Victoria Street, cut through a huddle of ancient houses in 1851, resembled the straight shots Haussmann was planning for his rebuilding of Paris, but many of the new streets were short, while the longer invariably meandered, and their buildings avoided Parisian uniformity. The new links were also often associated with slum clearance, reflecting a growing awareness of the appalling overcrowding and ill-health found in the central area's extensive pockets of poverty. The road-building projects were a direct if primitive solution. When New Oxford Street flattened London's most notorious slum, the St Giles Rookery, in 1844 *Punch* recorded 'the outcry of the unlucky rooks, a dismal caw – "Where shall we go?" and a mournful, very mournful echo answers, "Heaven only knows".'

The Victorians were their own harshest critics. For John Ruskin the streets of London in the 1860s were 'drains for the discharge of the tormented mob', and the whole of the metropolis was 'that great foul city ... rattling, growling, smoking, stinking – a ghastly heap of fermenting brickwork, pouring out poison at every pore'. Another critic sardonically described the streets lined with the latest revivalist styles as 'new London's museum of architectural masks', and of the social realities behind the masks the *Clapham Gazette* wrote in 1870: 'The boasted civilisation about which the comfortable classes are ever ready to speak as the climax of human progress is only a film or screen to conceal the most ferocious and savage instincts.' These and similar Victorian condemnations of their own architecture and society have to a great extent formed the twentieth century's picture of the nineteenth. The modernists' view of Victorian architecture is almost wholly based on the ideology developed by nineteenth-century theorists when they substituted technological appraisal for aesthetic judgment and rejected taste in favour of history, so that 'good' and 'bad' were superseded by 'progressive' and 'reactionary'. If nothing else, it is a tribute to the modernists' tenacity of mind that these nineteenth-century prejudices have remained their unchanged dogma for more than a century.

Classicists have also taken a dim view of the course of nineteenth-century design. Not only did architecture split from technology (presumably the two had previously been one) but also taste 'collapsed'. The beginning of characteristic Victorian richness, marked by the spread of the late neo-classic palazzo style in the 1840s with elaborate pedimented window surrounds

Opposite above: Marylebone High Street presents late nineteenth-century eclectic architecture in a sinuous street of medieval origin. The principles of Victorian 'street architecture' encouraged individuality and variety but recognized and respected the theme of spatial and historical continuity. Marylebone High Street and the medieval alignment of Marylebone Lane, nearby, have been excluded from adjacent Conservation Areas. One additional storey in the wrong place could obliterate views to the spire of St Marylebone. Unprotected view

Opposite below: Grosvenor Street changes alignment to meet the crossing of New Bond and Maddox Streets, leading to St George's, Hanover Square, which dominates the sequence for a half mile, as does St Marylebone in Marylebone High Street. Unprotected view

projecting on brackets, graphic mixture of brick and stucco, rusticated quoins, growing use of eclectic detail and general blurring of proportion, represents for classicists the 'collapse of the Georgian rule of taste'. Viewed in isolation as purely elevational compositions, Victorian palazzi certainly lack the elegant restraint and serene proportions of the terraces of the Golden Age, which ideally bounded Georgian squares and were meant to be seen as elevational architecture. The palazzo style and its even more elaborate successors had a different frame of reference, not to be found primarily in details of style or in systems of proportion but in the Victorian conception of townscape: 'street architecture' seen foreshortened and in movement, with the details of whatever style arranged to create changing patterns of textured intricacy, punctuated in the later nineteenth century by corner turrets and variegated rhythms of skyline. The development of Victorian architecture represents not a 'collapse of taste' but a change in its direction prompted by a different urbanistic context, and a different way of viewing it.

For nineteenth-century architects the most characteristic form of graphic representation was the eye-level perspective drawing, just as for the eighteenth century it was the elevation and section drawing, and for the twentieth it is the small-scale block model and the aerial view. Among the greatest of the nineteenth-century draughtsmen was A. W. N. Pugin, whose fascination with linear intricacy combined with his religious convictions made him the most outspoken of the early Victorian Gothicists. His vitriolic publications attacking pagan classicism and his design with Charles Barry of 1835 for the new Gothic Houses of Parliament introduced the 'Battle of the Styles' which George Gilbert Scott continued in his long dispute in the late 1850s with the classicist Lord Palmerston over Scott's design for the Foreign Office in Whitehall. Scott conceded defeat and produced a Florentine–Venetian design, but the conflict proceeded on other fronts. George Edmund Street's Gothic design for the Law Courts in the Strand published in 1868 drew the bitter scorn of both technologists and classicists.

St James's Street is composed of the kind of townscape ensembles which defy simple formulae. The Georgian and Victorian mixture of styles, materials, and buildings heights, are complemented by Norman Shaw's big asymmetrical corner block, in red brick and banded stone, which joins successfully with its neighbours despite its greater height

John Ruskin continued to denounce the 'foul torrent of the Renaissance' and into the 1870s architects produced designs in one style or the other, or both, according to their own convictions and the tastes of their clients. Thrusting commercial or industrial entrepreneurs could be expected to prefer the vernacular energy, technical ingenuity and display of workmanship of neo-Gothicism, and the vitality of George Gilbert Scott's St Pancras Station Hotel is as appropriate an expression of the Railway Age as the magnificent simplicity of the sheds behind. A crusading newspaper might choose the Gothic style and the clients of an insurance company might be soothed by ecclesiastical connotations, while those of aristocratic background or education might feel more at home surrounded by smooth classical erudition. Bankers invariably preferred their temples of Mammon in the timeless forms of classical antiquity. Gothic was never as popular as classic, but the two co-existed; one with sombre polychromatic brickwork and naturalistic ornament, the other laden with heavy festoons and with great projecting cornices, sometimes combined with balustrades and Parisian mansard roofs. Together they created the opulent 'pleasing gloom' of High Victorian architecture.

In 1863 *The Builder* announced: 'There is one prevailing idea – something large, coarse, showy, thick, clumsy, would be grand, but not an idea of England's sweet poetic loveliness and littleness.' A decade later Norman Shaw introduced the misnamed 'Queen Anne Revival' – a return to the domestic red-brick styles of the English seventeenth century and to fresh vivacity. The style, denounced in classical quarters as 'the very lowest state of corrupt erections', bearing marks of 'the senility of decaying taste', immediately proved popular and soon mixed with an amalgam of red-brick

Alfred Waterhouse's King's Weigh House Church, now the Ukrainian Church, and its setting in Mayfair are not part of a Conservation Area. The group shows the later Victorian fascination for skyline.
Unprotected view

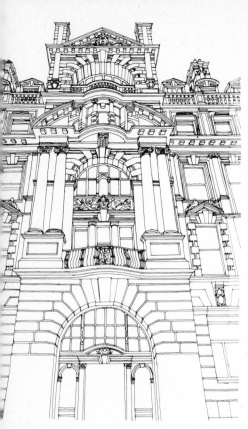

Telephone House in Temple Avenue (see Walk 5) is an example of the Edwardian Baroque inspired by seventeenth-century Italian designs and by works of Christopher Wren

and terracotta styles to spread over the West End. Eclecticism had invaded the classical citadel as well, and by the 1870s architects were producing freely-mixed and often inventive designs of the kind unloved by categorizers and systematizers.

Revivalist designs of the previous decades whether Gothic or classic often had a sombrely or primly moralistic flavour, while eclectic works seemed wilfully individualistic with a strain of hedonism suited to the great number of restaurants, cafés and theatres put up in the late 1870s and 1880s. The designs also showed an affinity with the Impressionist conception in their all-over use of detail and their disregard for unity and clarity of form. As architects grew more adept at their mixtures, the results often became genuinely epicurean and exquisite, dealing in visual timbre and nuances of mood.

Norman Shaw was the most influential architect of the later nineteenth century in London, and a master of richly varied pastiche. He also helped to lead the Baroque revival which coincided with the end of Queen Victoria's reign and the beginning of the Edwardian period. The scale of buildings had increased markedly during the Victorian era, but architects, regardless of their stylistic preferences, seem to have been determined to break down the apparent mass of their buildings by the use of intricate forms and rich, all-over décor, and by emphasizing a varied skyline. Edwardian designers sought to augment rather than diminish the impression of size by organizing and restricting the use of detail to produce large, blocky designs of smooth assurance which were more or less academically correct versions of the Italian Baroque, or more typically, of Christopher Wren's more exuberant works.

Throughout the course of Victorian revivalism and eclecticism, styles had been used in a literal or representational way to refer to the building's use or to the character or history of its area. Edwardian architects preferred to use styles abstractly for purely aesthetic reasons, often without any particular reference to the character of a building's use. Sometimes the results were incongruous, as in the London County Council's headquarters on the South Bank fitted out as an overblown château from the age of French absolutism.

Perhaps the most important contribution of Victorian and Edwardian architects to London's townscape resulted from their careful placement of picturesque features on the skyline. Major public buildings beginning with the early Victorian Houses of Parliament, followed by the High Victorian Law Courts in the Strand and the late Victorian Baroque Admiralty in Whitehall were all conceived in terms of angled street views and meandering vistas, breaking with Renaissance and Baroque symmetry and dispensing with the normal principles of elevational architecture to achieve their skyline effects. The order they produced, supplemented by countless designs responding sensitively to place and circumstance, resulted in a series of relationships more subtle and more apparently 'accidental' than the thoroughly predictable continental logic of majestic symmetrical monuments set in consistent geometric street layouts. Hundreds of thousands of Londoners living and working in the central area perceived these subtle relationships and developed the quiet awareness of their value which grew with familiarity. Yet architectural critics seemed unable to grasp the fundamental principles of nineteenth-century picturesque urbanism and even now continue to discuss nineteenth-century buildings individually in sterile ideological terms. The extent of the urbanistic catastrophe resulting from this discrepancy between ordinary perception and narrow specialist interests was reflected in the rage of Londoners as they saw familiar townscape groups and constellations being picked off one by one by marauding bands of developers and their architects, while each act of barbarism was accompanied by smooth assurances from Royal Academicians and Fine Arts Commissioners that what had been lost was of no architectural importance.

Bankers' Classic, Bankers' Georgian, and Modernist London

The gulf which separates the works of the Victorian and Edwardian periods from the designs which followed the First World War is most dramatically illustrated by the contrast between the opulent grandeur of the Victoria Memorial of 1911 on the Mall and the numb starkness of the Cenotaph war memorial of 1919 in Whitehall. Before the war interesting divergences from the Edwardian Baroque had begun to develop with steel-framed buildings in classical dress following the lead of Selfridges in Oxford Street with its three-storey bays of black metal and glass set in giant fluted colonnades. A chunky, aggressive Portland stone style with prismatic non-classical detail also made its appearance in Oxford Street and Piccadilly, but inventive tendencies seem to have been frozen by the impact of the war and by the subsequent official terror of mass rebellion. A truncated 'classicism', combining pomposity with meanness arose after the war, with mammoth, lumpish forms reflecting both the increasing scale and impersonality of commercial enterprises, and the Ecole des Beaux Arts system of architectural training, which concentrated on the quick conceptual sketch-design, or *parti*, demanded by the Prix de Rome competitions. Authentic classical detail could still be found on the Bankers' classic designs in the City of London, but even there the chastening effect of early modernists' propaganda could be sensed – the details appeared glued on as if ready to be stripped off by avenging purists. During the depression of the 1930s large-scale commercial and some residential redevelopment took place in parts of the West End. The style adopted was a paraphrase at greatly expanded scale of the red-brick domestic vernacular of the Queen Anne and early Georgian periods. From the point of view of townscape these simply adhered to street lines and obeyed the height limit of the 1888 Building Act's hundred-foot rule.

Modernism is a complex hybrid of geographically mixed descent. German architects during the years of social upheaval following the First World War echoed Victorian critics in their fixation upon methods and technological processes and joined them in rejecting the architectural inheritance of the Renaissance, but gave the English exhortations a Teutonic twist by substituting the morality of the machine for the integrity of medieval handicrafts, and the rectilinear economies of steel and glass for the harmonious vigour of Gothic construction. The flowering of the Bauhaus style in the 1920s was accompanied by the appearance of a Viennese mutation responding to Adolf Loos' dictum 'ornament is crime', and of the bi-plane views of Le Corbusier's Radiant City of point blocks and traffic interchanges. These formed the hard core of classic modernism which by the 1930s had gained critical acclaim and a measure of official acceptance on the Continent. Britain repelled the style which was to a large extent her own intellectual offspring until the 1950s when it returned to 'pass over Albion's cities' like 'the deluge of forgotten remembrances' in William Blake's *Jerusalem*.

It is particularly unfortunate that a generation of British architects, trained to look upon the traditional fabric of English townscape not as part of a historical continuum which included our own time, but as an antique curiosity, also lacked the basic visual awareness to see that modernism in its raw form could hardly be at home in the setting of English towns, and that a great deal of intelligent adaptation would be required if these works were to avoid being brutally disruptive.

The career of modernism in Britain has been brief and unhappy. Long resistance delayed its advent, but it arrived in the 1950s with a vengeance, preceded and accompanied by a ferocious critical and academic barrage which raked the defending philistine ranks with fusillades of scorn. As the modernists advanced in the 1960s their works were accompanied by a drumfire of design awards and rave reviews, and their chieftains were granted knighthoods. By the late 1960s when victory seemed in their grasp, a groundswell of embittered public resistance, aided first by the new

The Precinct north and west of St Paul's is typical of modernist schemes put up in the 1960s, with its relentless rectilinearity, 'flowing spaces', and truncated awareness of its surroundings

Conservation Area legislation and then by the collapse of the property boom in 1973, brought their advance to a virtual standstill.

Conservation Area legislation, which began in Parliament as a private member's bill, had its origins outside the professions of architecture and townplanning. It arose from an awareness that the townscape quality of an area may often far exceed the value of its buildings considered individually and that the monuments of traditional architecture were never intended solely as objects of isolated contemplation, but were to be seen and experienced in relation to their settings. It is not surprising that these homely truths were overlooked by a whole generation of architects who considered themselves conceptual thinkers rather than empirical observers.

One effect of conservation legislation and of public pressure has been increasing talk in the architectural profession of what they call 'contexturalism'. Another has been the annihilation of English Brutalism. The theorists of modernism blame the style's collapse on a 'failure of communication'. A more direct explanation would be that this thoroughly disagreeable style simply exceeded the limit of public tolerance. Its jagged concrete forms have been replaced by smooth surfaces of polished granite

Wren's brilliant assistant, Nicholas Hawksmoor, proposed a design for a piazza facing St Paul's which ingeniously brought the angled approach of Ludgate Hill into a symmetrical enclosure opening to the west front in broad curves similar to the present nineteenth-century frontages south-west of the Cathedral. Perhaps, when the time comes to demolish the Precinct, the principal approach to St Paul's intended by Wren and sketched by Hawksmoor will finally be respected

and one-way glass – a stylistic shift which might be described as the movement from Brutalism to 'slickism'.

There are in London a handful of modernist works which show a basic awareness of their surroundings, and a few which sensitively contribute to them. These will be pointed out in the course of the walks outlined on the following pages.

Before embarking on townscape walks for a look at London's 'showy evolutions of buildings', it would be wise to bear in mind Dr Johnson's sound advice. Although the taste for modest ensembles of non-pedigreed architecture has been dismissed by the modernist high priests as 'pop preservationism', there is a long and honourable tradition in Western art which takes another viewpoint, shared by the Naturalist artists and writers of the nineteenth century with the Dutch genre painters of the seventeenth. They direct our attention to the beauty found in ordinary prosaic reality, in mundane and seemingly trivial subjects. The areas of humble, pragmatic buildings and streets, unpretentious, intimate and filled with the colour of urban life may well be the irreplaceable surviving part of London's 'wonderful immensity'.

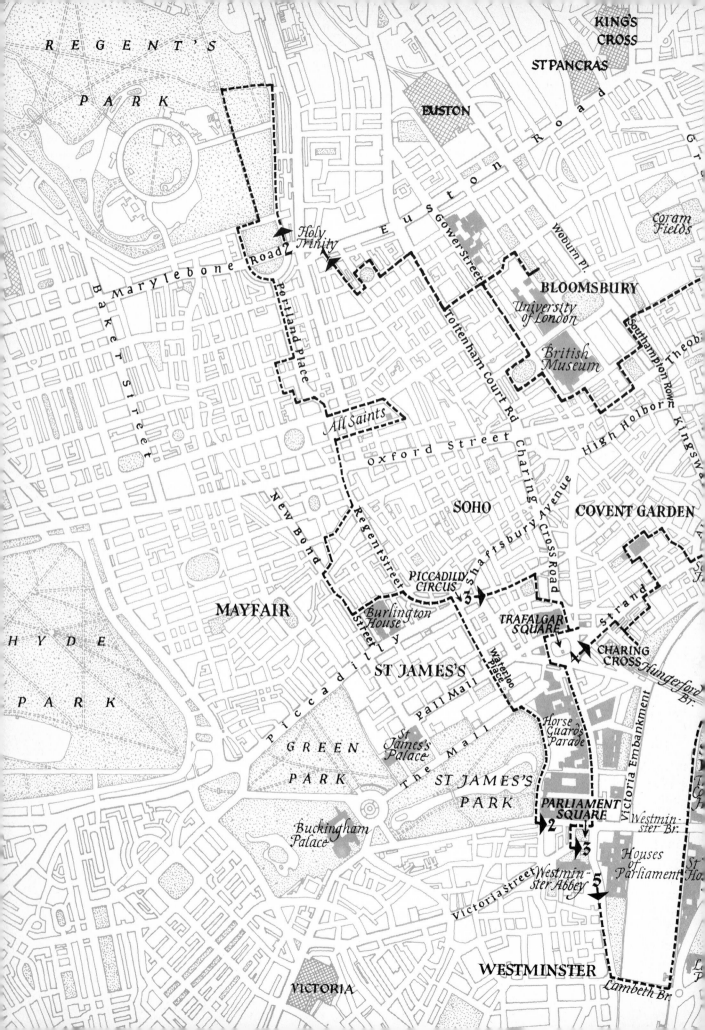

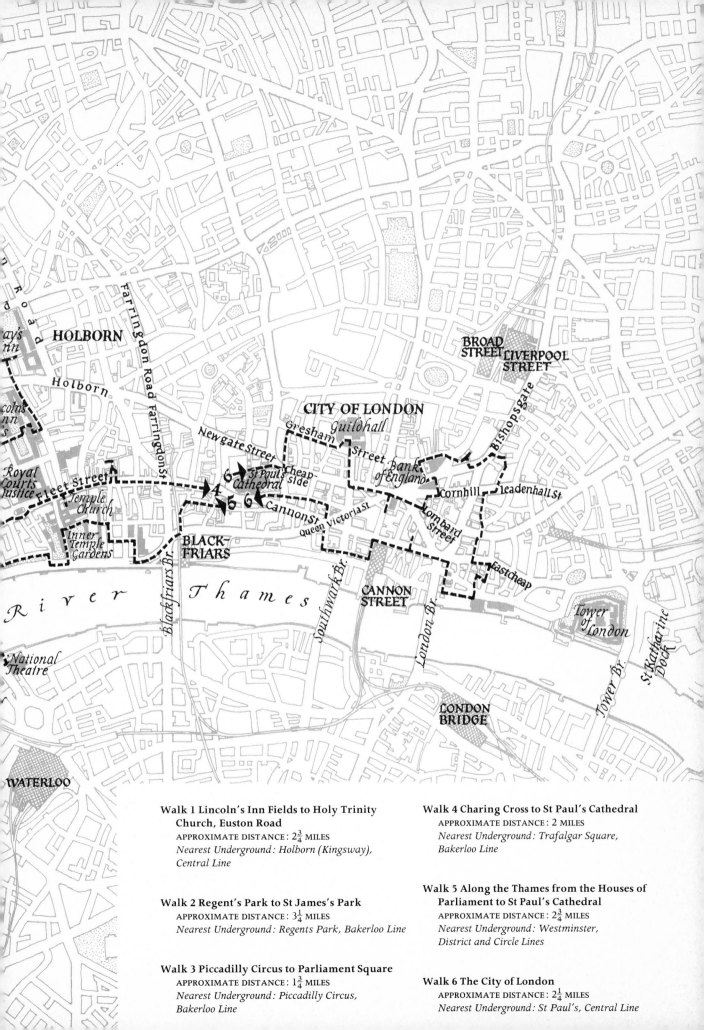

Walk 1 Lincoln's Inn Fields to Holy Trinity Church, Euston Road
APPROXIMATE DISTANCE: $2\frac{3}{4}$ MILES
Nearest Underground: Holborn (Kingsway), Central Line

Walk 2 Regent's Park to St James's Park
APPROXIMATE DISTANCE: $3\frac{1}{4}$ MILES
Nearest Underground: Regents Park, Bakerloo Line

Walk 3 Piccadilly Circus to Parliament Square
APPROXIMATE DISTANCE: $1\frac{3}{4}$ MILES
Nearest Underground: Piccadilly Circus, Bakerloo Line

Walk 4 Charing Cross to St Paul's Cathedral
APPROXIMATE DISTANCE: 2 MILES
Nearest Underground: Trafalgar Square, Bakerloo Line

Walk 5 Along the Thames from the Houses of Parliament to St Paul's Cathedral
APPROXIMATE DISTANCE: $2\frac{3}{4}$ MILES
Nearest Underground: Westminster, District and Circle Lines

Walk 6 The City of London
APPROXIMATE DISTANCE: $2\frac{1}{4}$ MILES
Nearest Underground: St Paul's, Central Line

Walk 1 Lincoln's Inn Fields to Holy Trinity Church, Euston Road

Lincoln's Inn Fields was the site of the Knights Templar's tilting ground until the dissolution of the Order in the early fourteenth century. It then became a recreation ground and promenade for local residents. During the first decades of the seventeenth century the Fields saw a series of running skirmishes between developers and the lawyers of Lincoln's Inn, who wished to preserve the open countryside and rural vistas west of the Inn. The lawyers won the first round, and in 1617 they commissioned Inigo Jones, then Surveyor-General to King James I, to lay out an 'ornamental walk' on the Fields in order to ward off further speculative schemes. Despite this, permission to build up the area was granted in 1638, provoking furious protests, including an appeal to the House of Commons by the lawyers of the Inn. As a compromise the centre portion of the site, the present Lincoln's Inn Fields, was left open. By the 1640s the south and west sides had been built up, not, as was the case ten years earlier at Inigo Jones' Covent Garden, as a unified architectural composition, nor, as in the Georgian squares a century later, as part of a larger townplanning scheme, but as a haphazard and apparently ramshackle operation.

No. 13 on the north side of the Fields is **Sir John Soane's Museum**. Soane, who designed the house and its neighbours on either side, was an influential, though eccentric designer whose work represents a break with the tradition of English classicism begun by Inigo Jones two centuries earlier. No. 13 was Soane's residence from 1813 until his death in 1837. The façade treats the rules of classicism with gentle irony: instead of pilasters and capitals, medieval brackets are slotted a third of the way up into grooves between the windows. Within the house the wry mannerisms continue and expand.

On the west side of the Fields **Lindsey House** (nos. 59–60) and its neighbour nos. 57–8 form a classical ensemble. Lindsey House, of about 1640, is thought to be a design of Inigo Jones. It was originally faced in brickwork with stone trim, but has been restuccoed and painted in the course of recent refurbishment. Nos. 57–8, of 1730, is the work of Henry Joynes, a loyal Palladian and member of Lord Burlington's architectural circle. The façade obviously pays respect to Lindsey House, but the straight pilasters alter the character of the composition compared with the slight convexity used by Jones. The semi-circular portico, added by Soane a century later, is a graceful addition to the rather starched correctness of the façade.

On the south side of the Fields the **Cancer Research Institute** occupies the site of a fine row of early Georgian houses pulled down in 1959. The **Royal College of Surgeons** next to it, like many of London's historic buildings, is a patchwork of compromises. It has a centre portion designed by Charles Barry in 1835, reusing the Ionic portico from a previous building on the site by George Dance, of 1806. The coherence of Barry's composition was lost with the construction of Victorian and twentieth-century additions above and on either side. At the south-east corner of the Fields the grim-looking neo-Jacobean **Land Registry**, built in 1911 on the site of Soane's Insolvent Debtors Court, would surely benefit from cleaning. Beyond, Serle Street frames a view south to the back of the Royal Courts of Justice, marked by the spire over the entrance hall in the Strand.

Lincoln's Inn lies east of the Fields. The arched gateway and the New Hall and Library north of it were designed by Philip Hardwick in 1843. The

New Square, Lincoln's Inn, dominated by the red-brick and banded stone rear tower of the Law Courts

romantic neo-Tudor design pays deference to the Inn's original architectural character. The presence of the Knights Templar a few hundred yards to the south originally attracted lawyers to the area in order to deal with cases arising over money matters, since the Templars, a military order, were also bankers to the nobility. Lawyers took up residence at Lincoln's Inn some time during the fourteenth century.

The Inn's rich variety of building styles and materials complements a sequence of green open spaces and paved courts laid out in additive medieval fashion. New Square, a seventeenth-century speculative development which subsequently became lawyers' chambers, bounds the Inn on the south. Beyond it the rear tower of the Courts of Justice rises impressively above the gatehouse to the square. Past the New Hall and Library on the left is a neo-Elizabethan building of the 1870s by George Gilbert Scott, with dark polychromatic brickwork and gables. North of it is the sparse, white classicism of Robert Taylor's Stone Buildings of 1774. Though the styles might be considered incompatible, the buildings in fact form a harmonious contrast, and together with Hardwick's New Hall they produce an effective townscape ensemble built up by three of London's finest architects over the course of a century. Old Square, rebuilt by Scott in the mid-1870s, is a paved space with a large plane tree at its centre. It forms a pleasant contrast with the grassed courtyard of the medieval Old Buildings and the Old Hall, 1492, which lie beyond the Tudor-arched undercroft of the Chapel, built in 1623.

Emerging from the restored gatehouse of 1518, through its original oak doors into Chancery Lane, the fairy-tale skyline of James Pennethorne's **Public Records Office**, 1851, appears to the south, while the street façades of Old Square and Stone Buildings accompany the walk north along Chancery Lane. We cross High Holborn, a medieval alignment now mostly built up with boring modern blocks, and proceed into Warwick Court, the entrance to **Gray's Inn**, founded in 1370. Gray's is the northernmost of the legal precincts which begin with the Temple on the Thames Embankment a

*No. 35 Bedford Row, a mid-eighteenth-
century house, is on the right.
Its neighbour on the left was built
about 1700, before fire codes forbade
heavy framed sash windows flush with
the wall*

half-mile to the south. We turn right at Gray's Inn Place into Field Court, a
paved area planted in pollarded plane trees particularly striking in winter.
Ahead is the entrance to the Hall of the Inn, 1560, and to Gray's Inn Square
and South Square, originally built in the late seventeenth century and
reconstructed after extensive war damage. An elegant wrought-iron gate
marks the entrance from Field Court to Gray's Inn Gardens, an impressive
green open space laid out around a formal axis with magnificent plane trees
planted, according to legend, by Francis Bacon. The Gardens are bounded on
the east by the red-brick backs of Gray's Inn Square and Verulam Buildings
of 1805, and on the west by Raymond Buildings of 1825; their dignified
repose and stately harmonies of proportion were achieved by means of an
absolute simplicity and regularity of layout, an economy of means, a
repetition of almost barracks-like architectural units, and a careful attention
to detail which never loses sight of the whole.

We return by way of Field Court to Gray's Inn Place, and from there
proceed by way of Bedford Place, with its seventeenth-century water pump,
to **Bedford Row**, begun by the notorious developer Dr Nicholas Barbon for
the Bedford Corporation in 1686. Barbon's plan of two years before to build
up Red Lion Square nearby had provoked the members of Gray's Inn, who,
like their colleagues at Lincoln's Inn half a century before, feared the loss of
their rural vistas. In desperate attempts to stop the development, the lawyers
of the Inn twice attacked Barbon's workmen in pitched battles, legal
remedies having failed. Barbon himself led the brickies in a victorious
charge, and the square was built.

Only two of his Bedford Row houses have survived, nos. 42–3. Barbon
went bankrupt and died a few years later, stipulating in his will that none of
his debts should ever be paid, thus continuing the principle by which he had
done business throughout his career. The rest of the street was developed
around 1700, and most of the original houses remain. They are of brown

brick, with red hand-rubbed brick dressings, and sometimes with keystones at the heads of the windows, the heavy frames of which are brought forward nearly flush with the external brickwork. These details are typical of early eighteenth-century terraces, as are the flat bracketed hoods over the doors, and the general absence of 'correct' proportions in the windows. An interesting exception is no. 35, which should be compared with its neighbour to the south, no. 36. No. 35 has the fully recessed, slender-framed sash windows and stuccoed surrounds to the inner face of the window openings which were required, as a fire precaution, by the Building Act of 1709. It does not appear as if this regulation was consistently enforced outside the City of London until the mid-eighteenth century, and no. 35 is probably of that period.

Raymond Buildings, Gray's Inn, in a setting of plane trees planted in the seventeenth century

The walk proceeds north along Bedford Row towards **Great James Street**. The two streets, separated by Theobalds Road, form a single, easily comprehensible corridor, visually closed at either end. Great James Street is a scaled-down version of Bedford Row, and an illustration of the simple Georgian rule of thumb, based on fire regulations, which apportioned the height of buildings according to the width of the street, which in turn influenced the proportions of the façade. The houses in Great James Street were built in the 1720s with the segmental window heads typical of that decade.

The vista along the street focuses upon **Rugby Chambers**, whose stuccoed façade, now dirty grey rather than white, forms a mid-Victorian contrast with the Georgian brick terraces which frame the view. The building is owned by the Rugby (School) Estate, and is in need of maintenance and repair. Its visual prominence results from the unmatched grids of adjoining estates, and because of its townscape importance it should be position listed.

The east side of **Millman Street** is an object lesson in non-conservation. A row of fine terraces which continued the style of Great James Street were acquired by Camden Council with the intention of pulling them down and constructing council houses in their place. Since the entire row of houses was listed, Camden seems to have used the developers' technique of planned decay, waiting patiently until, in 1971, a chimney pot fell into the street. Camden's district surveyor was rushed to the scene, where he displayed remarkably quick thinking: the whole east side of the street was immediately pulled down. Walkers will draw their own conclusions about what has been put up in its place.

Stung by criticism of this kind of 'conservation' Camden has since purchased houses nearby in **Great Ormond Street**, which it hopes to rehabilitate. Also in Great Ormond Street are some pragmatic and sympathetic Victorian modifications to this fine early eighteenth-century street: no. 2 is a late neo-classic stucco front, and nos. 6–8 a later Victorian paraphrase of its older neighbours.

Great Ormond Street crosses Lamb's Conduit Street, presenting a view to the north towards **Coram Fields**, which were laid out as the grounds for Thomas Coram's Foundling Hospital in 1739. The hospital was built in 1749–52, and demolished, after considerable protest, in 1926.

Queen Square, named after Queen Anne, and developed shortly after her death in 1714, was originally open to the north, with a pleasant view to the wooded hills of Hampstead. This was closed by the building of Guilford Street in the 1790s. Near the north end is a statue, not of Queen Anne as the Ministry of Works stoutly maintained for nearly a century, but of Queen Charlotte, consort to King George III. The southern portion of the square is paved, and has the quality of a piazza. On the south it is bounded, appropriately enough, by the Italian Hospital, an ornate Victorian Renaissance design by T.W. Cutler of 1898 which, by the law of opposites, goes well with the austere Stanhope Institute next to it. The Church of **St George the Martyr** forms the western edge of the 'piazza'. St George's Victorian Gothic façade has been wrapped around an Anglican Baroque interior. At least some of the interior has been restored to its original state.

Cosmo Place leads from Queen Square to Southampton Row, the eastern boundary of **Bloomsbury**. Bloomsbury's other boundaries are Holborn on the south, Tottenham Court Road on the west, and Euston Road on the north. Most of this district was originally developed by the Bedford Estate in the eighteenth and early nineteenth centuries. The subsequent additions of the British Museum, and then of the University of London at first altered, and then, in the latter case, destroyed not only the architectural coherence, but also the essentially residential character of Bloomsbury.

Before entering Bloomsbury Square the blank end wall in Southampton Row of nos. 1–5 Bloomsbury Place should be noted, for it suggests that this

Opposite above: Nash's speculative conversion of the corner block in Bloomsbury Square, until recently occupied by the Royal Pharmaceutical Society, was his architectural debut, and was also an early instance of the overall use of stucco

Opposite below: the 'piazza' of Queen Square is bounded on the south by the Italian Hospital and the Stanhope Institute

group of houses stucco-fronted in the mid-nineteenth-century palazzo style are of much earlier origin. In fact they were built in the 1670s, at the time when Bloomsbury Square was first developed. The Earl of Southampton, Lord Treasurer to Charles II, built his mansion, Southampton House, at the north end of the square in 1661. The other sides of the square were completed during the course of the next twenty years, while **Southampton Place**, an axial extension of the square to the south, and part of Southampton's original plan, was finished by Henry Flitcroft in the 1740s. The Earl of Southampton's estate passed by marriage to the Russell family, the dukes of Bedford.

In 1798 the Duke of Bedford decided to vacate Southampton House, demolish it, and construct on the fields to the north the series of squares and streets which gave Bloomsbury its distinctive character. In a bold scheme continuing Flitcroft's axis of Southampton Place, **Bloomsbury Square** was linked by a new street, Bedford Place, on the site of Southampton House, to Russell Square, largest of London's squares, landscaped by Humphry Repton and built by James Burton in 1800. The theme of axial balance was continued in the 1840s and 50s with the Victorian stucco-fronting of the original houses of the 1670s framing the Georgian replacements of Southampton House. The symmetry is emphasized by use of a London 'black and white' contrast – dark brick terraces set off by stucco façades on either side.

Other houses around the square have been modified or replaced, often with considerable skill. Nos. 16–17 on the west side are a rebuilding of 1777 by John Nash of the late seventeenth-century house originally occupied by the Earl of Northampton. The Royal Pharmaceutical Society again modified the building in 1857, adding a portico, the bracketed pediments over the windows, and a top storey. The centrepiece of the west side, the mid-Victorian stuccoed façades of nos. 9–14 also cover houses built nearly two hundred years earlier. No. 6 is what it appears to be, a Georgian house of about 1740.

The mammoth Liverpool Victoria Insurance building of 1928 overpowers the square on the east side. On the south side of the square, two attractive ranges of mixed eighteenth- and nineteenth-century buildings flank Southampton Place, the impressive and nearly intact composition of 'Burlington's Harry' Flitcroft. Lord Burlington with Flitcroft and the rest of his Palladian coterie were the arch-rivals of Nicholas Hawksmoor, possibly the greatest of the English Baroque architects. Hawksmoor's **St George's, Bloomsbury**, in Bloomsbury Way to the west of the square, was one of the Fifty Churches authorized by the new Tory and High Church government in the 1711 Act of Parliament, intended to remedy the acute shortage of churches resulting from London's rapid expansion. Of the Fifty Churches, twelve were actually built, six of them by Hawksmoor. The church was begun in 1716 and when completed after delays in 1731 it was denounced by the Palladians as 'ridiculous even to a proverb'. Flitcroft prepared a detailed list of defects for the Church Commissioners.

St George's is best approached along the south side of Bloomsbury Way, in order to appreciate the powerful effect of the portico and the steeple. The former, with its giant order of Roman Corinthian columns, has been set back from the street and raised on a high podium, making it 'the most imposing church entrance in London'; the latter is surely the oddest steeple. It was based on the Mausoleum of Halicarnassus, with King George I at the top in place of King Mausolus.

The Commissioners had stipulated in regulations accompanying the Fifty Churches Act that all sanctuaries were to be oriented on the traditional east–west axis. Hawksmoor accommodated this arrangement with great ingenuity on a difficult site. However, by 1781 the continuing growth of the parish required the installation of additional seating, and the replanning of the interior. The altar was shifted to the north end of the church and the entrance to the great portico on the south, where they have remained since.

In the nineteenth century, the church was restored by G.E. Street, the architect of the Royal Courts of Justice in the Strand. Although Street was a dedicated Gothicist, he was sympathetic to Hawksmoor's Baroque conception, and restored St George's interior as far as possible 'to comply with the original intention'.

Museum Street leads from Bloomsbury Way to the British Museum. After the Second World War, the Royal Academy proposed clearing an axial approach to the museum from St George's. It may have been an interesting idea to connect the two monuments, but it was hardly worth the pulling down of whole streets of sound, useful and uniquely attractive buildings which had been refronted in a Parisian style by the Bedford Estate between 1857 and 1862.

The steeple of St George's Bloomsbury, familiar from Hogarth's Gin Lane, *was Hawksmoor's adaptation of a Wren proposal for surmounting the west dome of his Great Model design for St Paul's. Wren, in turn, derived the form from Pliny's description of King Mausolus' tomb. Mausolus' statue was finally discovered in the 1850s and transported to the British Museum, around the corner*

Smirke's monumental colonnaded façade of the British Museum reproduced on a much larger scale the Ionic proportions and details of Erechtheion in Athens

The Royal Academy plan may now seem to have been a harmless paper exercise, but along with other prestigious depreciation of the area, it encouraged the formulation of the National Library scheme, by Leslie Martin and others, to pull down the entire district south of the museum, a rich and varied mixture of shops, restaurants, book stores and residences, and replace it with a monolithic book warehouse for specialist scholars. A new site for the library was found near St Pancras Station, and the scheme was finally dropped in 1975 mainly as a result of the spirited opposition of the Bloomsbury Residents Association, aided by the GLC Historic Buildings Board, and later by Camden Council. But a decade of uncertainty induced by the plan took its toll: improvements in the area were frozen, businesses and residents moved out, and buildings decayed.

The approach to the main entrance of the **British Museum**, designed by Robert Smirke for George IV and built from 1823 to 1847, shows clearly that Smirke accepted the presence of houses facing the museum in Great Russell Street, and did not require their removal for his colonnaded front to be appreciated. The pedimented central portico has been set well back of strongly projecting wings on either side, creating a forecourt from which the Ionic proportions can be seen at a proper distance.

The austere nineteenth-century conception of classical Greece, embodied in the museum's Ionic colonnades and in its stern geometry, reflects the ideals by which the rising class of commercial and industrial entrepreneurs wished to be known: sober rationality, correctness and solid consistency. However well the museum may now seem to have represented the values of its time, it was the subject of sharp criticism from its contemporaries, not only because its neo-classic purity was out of fashion by the time the building was completed, but also because the architect had failed to make full and 'honest' use of the building technologies then available to him. Professor James Fergusson, a Victorian spiritual ancestor of our own technological fetishists, was bitingly critical of the museum's 'archaeological' façade, and querulously demanded to know why the building had not been constructed according to an eminently practical system of brickwork domes supported on cast-iron beams as used at a flaxmill in Leeds. The professor neglected to mention that his favourite mill had been clad externally as an Egyptian temple.

Leaving the museum, the graphic pattern of red brickwork and stone and many-gabled silhouette of **Great Russell Mansions**, 1888–96, form a lively counterpoint to the sombre columns which frame their view. Sir John Summerson has said of these buildings facing the British Museum that 'a cat may look at a king'. Indeed, and the 'cat' should be position listed.

Returning to Great Russell Street and proceeding towards Bloomsbury Street, one passes buildings opposite the museum which have also thus far happily survived the scorn of classical opinion – the stucco pastries of the Museum Tavern and no. 48 west of it, and the scaled-down palazzo fronts of nos. 43–7.

Bedford Square lies north of Great Russell Street along Bloomsbury Street, and is the finest and most nearly intact of London's Georgian squares. It was designed in 1774 by Thomas Leverton for the widow of the Earl of Bedford as a unified large-scale speculative layout with middle-class clients in mind, following the lead set by Robert Adam a few years earlier at the Adelphi south of the Strand (see Walk 4). The features which unify the buildings around the square are the distinctive pattern of alternated rusticated stone and brickwork around the entrances, with bearded heads at the keystones, the stuccoed centrepieces varying in width from three to six bays in the middle of each terrace, and the balustraded cornices at their ends. The paraphrased Ionic capitals supporting the pediments of each terrace's centrepiece, and the famous door surrounds are also found, respectively, in the Adams' Portland Place and New Cavendish Street Houses (see Walk 2). The details may have been designed by a young Italian draughtsman who appears to have worked for both Leverton and the Adam Brothers.

The terraces around the square are constructed according to building regulations drawn up in 1774 by William Chambers, Robert Taylor and George Dance. The houses step down in size from 'first' to 'third' rate as set out in the regulations, and the resultant variation of the roofline distinguishes Bedford Square from neo-classic squares of the Regency period with their uniform cornices. The 1774 building code was one aspect of the Georgian 'age of improvements' – others were the acts specifying road widths, street lighting, and details of paving. The Chambers/Taylor/Dance code set out the proportions of façades according to Palladian ratios, and prescribed the specifications of materials and details of construction in a way which left nothing to the imagination. The magnificent architecture of the Georgian 'Golden Age' was thus the direct result of the strictest legal regulation and of the use of absolutely standardized building components. Modernists who complain that rigid building codes and industrialized parts prevent aesthetic expression should ponder this.

The square was enhanced in 1975 when Camden Council banned all car-parking and widened the pavements. On the west side behind the elegant façade of nos. 35–6 is the Architectural Association, founded in 1847, and located here since 1917. The Association has offered a full-time course of architectural study since 1901, and over the years has been a centre of ferment. In the 1930s it was the semi-official headquarters of the MARS group of militant modernists, and its graduates continue as the trend-setters of contemporary British architecture.

Gower Street, north of Bedford Square, was 'utterly intolerable' to George Gilbert Scott and for John Ruskin it was the *ne plus ultra* of ugliness in street architecture. The unadorned flat planes of Georgian streets and the uniformity of their details outraged the Victorians. The typical blank end walls of a Georgian terrace, as at the corners of Gower and Chenies Streets, must have particularly incensed later nineteenth-century architects, for whom a corner site was an obvious occasion for lavish display. The Georgian system of construction employed heavy end walls to brace an entire terrace, preventing the 'domino effect'. With improved engineering techniques the Victorians achieved bracing in other ways. Cast-iron construction, in some cases, and a more precise understanding of the strength of materials, as well as more exact methods of calculating loads, all allowed greater freedom in the shaping of a building's outer shell.

At the south-east corner of Gower Street and Torrington Place a wild Flemish-Gothic extravaganza by Fitzroy Doll, dated 1907, with rabid-looking gargoyles thrusting from its façade, marks the entrance into the territory of the **University of London**. To the east, from the north end of Torrington Square, one may obtain a view of the kind of development with which the university planners have replaced the elegant, linked squares and leafy vistas which once made Bloomsbury unique, and no doubt did much to attract the Bloomsbury Group, and the Pre-Raphaelites before them. The present series of monolithic blocks culminates in the massive pile of **Senate House**, inexplicably allowed to slip past the London height limit still in force in the 1930s, and recently even more inexplicably listed by the architectural scholars of the Department of the Environment. Those walkers who wish to savour in full the impact of the university upon the once civilized townscape of Bloomsbury may further penetrate the groves of academe into what remains of Woburn Square.

The ruined stump of **Christ Church, Woburn Square**, lies at the feet of Sir Denys Lasdun's Institute of Education and Advanced Legal Studies. The church, an early example of the Gothic revival in London, was designed by Lewis Vulliamy in 1831, with fine altar panels by Edward Burne-Jones. Christina Rossetti, sister of Dante Gabriel Rossetti, founder of the Pre-Raphaelite Brotherhood, worshipped here. Its parish destroyed by the expanding university, Christ Church became redundant, then 'unsafe' and finally in 1974 it was pulled down at the insistence, so the Commissioners maintain, of Camden's district surveyor. The working relationship between the Church Commissioners and the district surveyor has continued – in 1977 it resulted in the demolition of St Matthew's, Oakley Square, without the demolition notice required by law ever reaching the borough council. Camden's planning officers explained that the notice was 'lost'. For their role in the affair the Church Commissioners were presented with a 'Black Award for Environmental Vandalism' by the Save Britain's Heritage organization.

The expansion of the Institutes of Education and Advanced Legal Studies seems thus far to have stumbled over the corpse of Christ Church, since an act of Parliament is required to permit its change of use. For two years after its demolition the old church noticeboard still hung by the ruined entrance offering 'a special welcome to overseas visitors'.

After returning to Gower Street, the walk continues west along Torrington Place to Tottenham Court Road. Approaching it, two gigantic silhouettes loom into view: first the **Post Office Tower**, a straightforward folly with its revolving restaurant, 579 feet high and visually intriguing in its space-age way; then comes Joe Levy's **Euston Centre**, a marked-down version of a Manhattan speculator's block, 408 feet high and of no architectural interest. It does, however, show how government agencies seem willing to take the risk out of speculation by filling otherwise unwanted office space. In the case of Euston Centre, the Post Office and other government departments have amply rewarded Mr Levy's speculative shrewdness.

Grafton Way, leading to **Fitzroy Square**, displays a row of good second-rate Georgian houses in various states of disrepair. The square was begun by Robert Adam in 1793 and is bounded on the south and east by two blocks which he designed to appear as single buildings, more or less successfully disguising rows of identical houses behind large-scale façades, elaborating upon the kind of unity produced by Thomas Leverton at Bedford Square

twenty years before. There the identity of each house was still clearly marked by its striking door surround. Adam handled the proportions of these large façades, particularly of the eastern block, with great skill. The north and west sides of Fitzroy Square were built thirty to forty years after Adam's first terraces in a stucco style which echoes the buildings of Regent's Park nearby. Except for a graceless early twentieth-century intruder on the north side, the buildings around the square are externally intact, while the skyline belongs to the Post Office and Joe Levy. Fitzroy Square has benefited from Camden's pedestrianization scheme of 1976.

Throughout the nineteenth and into the early twentieth century the 'Fitzrovia' area north of Soho from Percy Street to Fitzroy Square attracted artists and writers. Among those who lived here were Constable, Bonington, Whistler, and in Fitzroy Square, Madox Brown and Virginia Woolf. The southern portion of 'Fitzrovia' is now the centre of London's Greek and Turkish Cypriot community, while the northern part, including the square, has been mainly taken over by offices.

Cleveland Street, west of Fitzroy Square, marks a boundary of some importance. It is an urban 'seam', stitching up the difference between the layouts of adjoining estates: the Bedford–Fitzroy grid of Bloomsbury and 'Fitzrovia', and the Harley/Portland Estate grid following the alignment of Portland Place. Before the development of these estates, Cleveland Street was a broad and prominent rural avenue known as the Green Lane. In medieval times it had been the boundary of the Tottenhall Manor with adjoining farmsteads, and it may well have had its genesis in that legendary origin of London streets, the cow path. Cleveland Street is now the boundary between the Borough of Camden and the City of Westminster.

One need not present travel documents when crossing the street, nonetheless it represents a division with an appreciable effect upon the townscape, and upon the lives of local residents. As a typical London border landscape the area has attracted the less remunerative and prestigious kinds of use: originally cabinet makers and joiners employed in fitting out the Regents Park terraces lived here. It is now occupied by working-class residences, small local shops and restaurants, and workshops. These, in turn, seem to draw irresistibly schemes for speculative redevelopment, and

Thomas Leverton's Bedford Square houses display the variation in size allowed for in the Building Regulations of 1774

Fitzroy Square is dominated on the north by Euston Centre, and on the south by the Post Office Tower

because of the 'untidy' mixture of uses and the humble buildings which house them, they also invariably inspire local authority 'slum clearance' projects.

The effect of the differing policies of Camden and Westminster upon the physical fabric of such an area can be seen in sharp relief in Cleveland Street and in houses nearby. The east side of the street, in Camden, is part of the Fitzroy Square Conservation Area, and because of this its modest Georgian buildings and their uses – shops, residences and even an English restaurant – have remained intact and even thrive in their quiet way, free from the threat of total clearance schemes. Across the street, in Westminster, a whole row of Victorian houses, Regent's Park Mansions, 1898, have been pulled down, and their site awaits development; while a block of twenty listed, structurally sound Georgian houses in adjoining Carburton, Great Titchfield and Greenwell Streets stand under the threat of compulsory purchase and demolition.

The north end of Cleveland Street meets **Euston Road**, originally laid out as London's 'outer ringway' in 1757. By the early nineteenth century, London had already begun to spread north of the New Road, as it was then known, most significantly with the development of Regent's Park. Three important churches of the neo-classic period were sited along the New Road – the archaeologically correct Greek Revival St Pancras Parish Church of 1819, the late Palladian St Marylebone Church of 1812, framed in a neo-classic vista, and **Holy Trinity Church** of 1828 by John Soane. Walkers may wish to compare at their leisure the similarities and striking differences of the three churches. Holy Trinity, like St Marylebone, breaks with the traditional east–west orientation and is sited on a visually-dictated north–south axis. To appreciate the importance of this change, Hawksmoor's efforts a century before to maintain the conventional orientation on a nearly impossible site in Bloomsbury should be recalled. By the 1820s architects were quite willing to sacrifice the fundamental symbolic principle of church design in order to achieve a visual ideal, or to follow the dictates of fashion.

Soane was a master of scholarly eclecticism. His details appear as quotations from works of archaeological research, often historically and symbolically incongruous, as the Egyptian palm-leaf capitals supporting Holy Trinity's cupola, or unheard-of in classical terms, as the meander pattern across the entablature of the portico, a theme also found on the façade of his house in Lincoln's Inn Fields.

Little of Soane's work remains in central London. His masterpiece, the Bank of England, was made unrecognizable in the 1930s; his Westminster Law Courts, Royal Entrance to the House of Lords and Board of Trade in Whitehall have all more or less vanished. Holy Trinity remains as the personal statement of an extraordinarily inventive designer. The interior of the church has been converted to offices.

Walk 2 begins at Park Square East.

Close examination of Holy Trinity Church will show how Soane's eclectic choice of column capitals has converted the realities of load and support into visual poetry: billowing Ionic swirls below, then knuckled late Roman floral capitals, and at the top graceful palm leaves springing effortlessly upward. The proportions of tower and cupola hint at the growing Gothic Revival

Walk 2 Regent's Park to St James's Park

The route mainly follows John Nash's great townplanning scheme built between 1812 and 1827 for the Prince Regent, later George IV. There have been a good many grandiose London plans, some equalling Nash's in boldness, but none except his was actually built in a form approximating the original intention. The execution of the scheme can be attributed to Nash's close relationship with the Regent, a man of considerable culture, ambition and appetite, and to the architect's personal dedication and sense for compromise. The project was London's first 'comprehensive redevelopment', driving a ceremonial way through densely built-up areas to connect the Prince Regent's residence at Carlton House with a proposed royal pleasure pavilion two miles to the north in a new park sited on Crown land in St Marylebone made available by the expiration of the Duke of Portland's lease in 1811. The plan's unified conception and vast scale embodied the Regent's vision of London as a capital city equal to Napoleon's Paris, and Tzar Alexander's St Petersburg. However strong the Regent's despotic urges may have been, they were tempered by a sceptical Parliament, and an increasingly astringent Treasury. London's great neo-classic composition avoids the unbending geometry of absolutism; its graceful curves and gentle changes of alignment are often the result of adjustment to land acquisition costs, and point to Nash's design skill in coaxing circumstance into conformity with an aesthetic ideal both 'classical' and 'picturesque'.

The fusion of the two can be seen and felt in **Regent's Park**, where a romanticized version of the architecture of classical antiquity encloses an equally romanticized representation of the English countryside. The park was in a way the culmination of the Georgian era of square-building; it tied together and expanded upon architectural themes which had been developing since the mid eighteenth century, among them the use of the Greek classical orders in long colonnades on vast palatial façades, a fondness for picturesque landscaping, grand vistas, and stucco. 'Roman cement' as it was then called had already been used selectively by Thomas Leverton and the Adam brothers, at Bedford Square and in Portland Place. It had the advantages of being particularly effective in London's often shadowless light, of lending itself to the neo-classic conception of antiquity as something pure, timeless and ghostly white, and of being decidedly cheaper than Portland stone.

The park is approached from Park Square East. Nash's **Albany Terrace**, 1823, with an Ionic colonnade faces **Park Square**, originally planned by him as a crescent completing the circle of Park Crescent to the south. North of Albany Terrace is a group bounded on the south by St Andrew's Terrace and on the east by St Andrew's Place with an engaged Corinthian portico terminating the vista from the Outer Circle to the west. The dominant building of the ensemble is Denys Lasdun's **Royal College of Physicians**, 1964. Lasdun's design is a study in sensitive contrasts, and is perhaps the finest London example of an 'uncompromisingly modern' building contributing to an historic composition without paraphrasing the forms or materials of its neighbours. North of the College is **Cambridge Gate**, 1875, a Second Empire design by Archer and Green, and beyond it, and in need of maintenance, is **Cambridge Terrace**, an odd Nash work of 1825.

Chester Terrace, the longest frontage in the park, was designed by James Burton in 1825. With neo-classic singlemindedness, Burton held the building

A view of Cumberland Terrace, Nash's masterpiece facing Regent's Park

The central London skyline seen from Broad Walk in the park

dead level throughout its nearly thousand-foot length despite the rising ground, thus sinking the entrance level at the north end nearly a storey below grade. The stern, vertically emphasised projecting pavilions at either end are impressively proportioned.

Tree-framed views of Nash's best work on the park, **Cumberland Terrace**, 1826, are obtained by entering the park at Chester Gate Walk and proceeding across the playing fields to Broad Walk. As we move north, Chester Terrace's low-lying silhouette is punctuated by the needle spire of James Pennethorne's **Christ Church, Albany Street**, 1838. Cumberland Terrace is made up of three blocks linked by Ionic triumphal arches. Flat entablatured Ionic porticos at the ends of each block punctuate the basic rhythm of a continuous run of giant order Ionic pilasters. The composition comes together in a grand ten-columned balustraded portico, behind which rises a heavily populated Grecian-sculptured pediment – a masterly piece of stage scenery. North of Cumberland Terrace, St Katherine's Hospital, 1828, signals the Gothic Revival.

We turn south at Broad Walk for a look at the skyline, and return to Park Square along a formal, tree-lined promenade in an otherwise picturesquely designed setting. The skyline south of the park has been shattered by series of grossly-conceived office blocks, crushing the sense of pastoral calm and laconic expanse which Nash intended.

Park Square West leads past **Ulster Terrace**, mirroring Albany Terrace across the square, to Euston (Marylebone) Road and on to **Park Crescent**, 1812, Nash's memorable connection between Regent's Park and Portland Place. Nash graced the crescent with a one-storey portico. Its paired, unfluted Ionic columns and plain, balustraded entablature have been shaped and detailed for the moving eye. The sense of procession is the result of a continuously evolving vista, unlike the axial line of march demanded by continental and later English neo-classicism.

The unusual width of **Portland Place** was determined by an Act of Parliament obtained by Lord Foley to ensure the protection of his view north

Disrespect for fine works of traditional architecture occurred before the arrival of hard-line modernism in London. Considerable havoc was wrought in the 1920s and 30s, some of the worst of it in Portland Place

The sweep of Park Crescent is one of the most irresistible parts of Nash's grand scheme

to the hills of Hampstead from Foley House at the south end of the street. Portland Place was built by the Adam brothers in the 1770s with first-rate Georgian houses in unified terraces around Foley's corridor. It was incorporated by Nash as a part of the ceremonial way from Carlton House to the park. Each Adam block was a symmetrical design framed by end pavilions, with an engaged stucco portico at the centre, rusticated stucco at the ground floor, elegant wrought-iron railings, and tiers of heavy, moulded string courses. The form of the entire street was built up through the repetition and symmetrical procession of these details, like a Mozart composition. Each block had its mirror image across Portland Place, while the design along the whole length of the street was balanced about the blocks in the centre. The unified consistency of the streetscape must have been enforced by the insistent perspective of the string courses. The effect was lost with the redevelopment of much of the street in the stripped-down and voluminous Portland stone style of the 1920s and 30s, but one can still gain a taste of the original design from what remains of it.

On the west side at the north end of Portland Place adjoining Park Crescent are nos. 77–81, a plain terrace built during the recession following the American Rebellion. A rich contrast is the earlier no. 75, an Adam house with fine vermiculated rustication at the ground floor, a cornice with delicate dentils, and Chambers/Taylor/Dance proportions overall. South, across Devonshire Street, the Turkish Embassy is a later Victorian paraphrase of Adam themes, and nos. 59–67 have a mid-nineteenth-century palazzo front on the original fabric. Nos. 59–67 is the surviving part of an Adam terrace, but it has been hacked at in a manner hard to believe: a fifth of the pediment has been sawn off and a pilaster split down the middle to make room for its nondescript neighbour of the 1930s. The decaying stuccoed Chinese

Embassy at Weymouth Street is a remaining end pavilion; its Ionic capitals recall those at Bedford Square.

Facing the embassy across Portland Place is an abstract-looking Portland stone block by Grey Wornum of 1932. It has curiously cringing figures carved above and flanking the entrance – the headquarters of the **Royal Institute of British Architects**. Between Weymouth and New Cavendish Streets are the two relatively complete ranges which were the centrepieces of the street. Both terraces have Victorian added storeys and have suffered war damage or partial replacement. The eastern block displays a variety of brick – yellow London stocks, greys, browns and some red-rubbed sections over the windows. The pedimented centre portion was the culmination of the scheme. It merits attention for its unusual recessed entrances, for its elaborate late-Roman capitals on straight pilasters, and its arabesque frieze across the entablature. The door surrounds and fanlights of these blocks are relatively subdued. Considering the financial difficulties encountered by the Adams in the course of building Portland Place, it seems sensible that richer decoration was confined to a position high up the façade where it would be best appreciated in a street of this width.

The walk turns west into New Cavendish Street, but before leaving Portland Place, no. 32 on the east side, a Victorian palazzo with elaborate window surrounds, and no. 28, a crisply restrained Adam centrepiece, should be mentioned. No. 28 and its mirror image opposite, no. 21, are surviving twins of the lopped-off pediment six hundred feet to the north. **New Cavendish** and **Mansfield Streets** present Adam houses on a smaller scale in more intimate surroundings. The tiered string courses disappear, the detail comes down to eye level and is treated with great delicacy. Nos. 61–3 New Cavendish Street have Bedford Square surrounds in triplicate, as a focus for the view from Mansfield Street, and hooded wrought-iron balconies of the nineteenth century on heavy brackets. Mansfield Street has a series of fine door designs; nos. 13–15 have particularly rich fanlights. The view south from Mansfield Street to Queen Anne Street presents a picture rather different from that to the north. Nos. 9–11 Queen Anne Street, Georgian houses with Victorian window surrounds, have been sandwiched between a 'low profile' 1970s design – two glum, fortress-like blocks surrounded by a decidedly uninviting concrete glacis reminiscent of the American Embassy's anti-riot device in Grosvenor Square. The buildings' entrances should be compared with the civilized Georgian doorways nearby.

Chandos House to the north-east is a stone-fronted design by Robert Adam of 1771. The portico has been finely carved with Greek and late Roman detail: the entablature presents rams' heads, festoons and rosettes; the arabesque design of palmettes derived from the Erechtheion was later repeated at larger scale in Portland Place. Here it is wrapped around the capitals.

Turning east into Portland Place from Chandos Street we return to Nash's design. **All Souls, Langham Place**, was the device by which he visually accommodated the change in alignment between Portland Place and his new Regent Street which had to bypass Foley House and properties on the east sides of Cavendish and Hanover Squares to the south. The design and placement of All Souls showed how well Nash was able to solve a problem by moving around it. The architectural effect of the circular portico and the needle spire above on a colonnaded drum has been diminished by over-scaled buildings later constructed nearby: the huge Victorian Langham Hotel on the site of Foley House, Broadcasting House to the north and the St George's Hotel to the south-east. As Regent Street now has little genuine architectural interest, we shall leave it for diversions on either side.

All Saints, Margaret Street, by William Butterfield may be reached by turning east from Regent Street into Mortimer Street. The district east of Langham Place now occupied by London's garment trade was first built up during the eighteenth century in comfortably scaled streets lined with

smaller Georgian houses. These were largely replaced toward the end of the nineteenth century with modest commercial structures. The consistent use of emphasized Victorian corners seems particularly well suited to the Georgian grid. 'The George', a High Victorian pub at the north-west corner of Mortimer and Great Portland Streets, diagonally faces Barclay's Bank, in an eclectic salmon-red-brick style of the 1890s. The corner buildings in the district are generally unlisted since their impurity is still frowned upon by official taste, and this is not a conservation area, because of its variety.

Wells Street is a diagonal alignment marking the boundary between the Portland and Berners Estates. South of Mortimer Street, **St Margaret's House**, a bold simple building of 1931 by Richardson and Gill, makes effective use of its prominent site at the bend in Wells Street which terminates the vista from Margaret Street to the west, by using a row of three-storey-high panels of glass with black metal frames and spandrels, set in a plain white-brick façade.

All Saints, Margaret Street, is a powerfully expressive Gothic Revival Church of 1851. The famous patterned exterior brickwork and coloured interior tiles and the gradation of structural forms and details inside and out have been drawn together to produce an awesome sense of scale which underlines much of the building's emotional impact. Attempting to explain it, critics have referred to the church's 'Dickensian cruelty', to its 'ugliness' and even to its 'sado-masochism'. Nikolaus Pevsner must have come closest to describing Butterfield's intention with his remark that 'from everywhere the praise of the Lord is drummed into you'.

The first impressions of the church from Margaret Street are of the remarkable patterned brickwork and of the tall buttressed tower surmounted by a chamfered green slate spire. The brickwork – an almost fanatical display of vernacular workmanship made up of dark reds and vitrified blues in alternate bands below and of diapered crosswork and chevrons with stone inserts above – is a forceful rejection of both smooth classical erudition and polite Tudor scholarship.

The church is entered through a free-standing arched gateway into a forecourt dominated by the great steeple and an asymmetrically placed 'buttress'.

The interior of the church is dominated by the decoration of the floor, the walls of the nave, the spandrels between arches, and the ceiling with its graphically emphasized beams and rafters. The predominant colour throughout is rust-red, set off with cream-yellow, orange, pale blue-green and black, seen in light filtered through the stained glass of the clerestory and the west window. The generous nave arches, supported on polished granite ribbed columns with varying foliage capitals, appear even larger due to the effect of their patterned spandrels, and of the intense rhythm of the roof beams, half of them non-structural, which give the nave a sense of scale far exceeding its modest size.

Returning along Margaret Street and crossing Oxford Circus, we approach the only block which seems to display a sense of position and makes good use of a theme of the original street, a late Victorian work: **Regent House** (nos. 236–41) of 1898 by G.D. Martin. Its copper pavilion dome and cupola mark the change in direction by which Nash brought his scheme into line with the old position of Swallow Street, thereby avoiding the houses around Golden Square and allowing room for the sweep into Piccadilly Circus of the Quadrant, as that curved part of Regent Street was known. This alignment also adroitly opened the west front of St Thomas' Church, 1702, into Regent Street. The church was restored by William Butterfield in 1872, and became the site of a car park in 1973.

The blocks of large-scale commerce march on to the Quadrant. We leave them at Maddox Street, drawn by the domed lantern tower of **St George's, Hanover Square**, an Anglican Baroque design of 1720 by John James. The heavy masonry blocks of the Maddox Street elevation and the six-columned portico facing St George's Street, similar to the design of 1716 for St George's, Bloomsbury, point to James' allegiance with Nicholas Hawksmoor in their battle against the Palladians. James' portico, with columns actually larger than Hawksmoor's, has a less grandiose effect. Hawksmoor's portico was set back from the street on a great podium, while James' entrance, conceived as a gateway to Hanover Square, projects into the narrow end of the splayed street south of the square on a slightly raised base, giving a sense of invitation and even intimacy, subtly enforced by the widened inter-columnation framing the centre entrance.

Immediately south of St George's is no. 31, an example of the mature north German Baroque style of the 1720s which made this street unique in London – red brick, high well-proportioned windows and moulded segmented heads and surrounds in stone, rusticated panels above and below the windows, equal quoins at corners, and big, fully moulded cornices. The smaller and more reticent English style of the period is found opposite: nos. 8–10 resemble houses in Great James Street (see Walk 1). North of the church on the west side of St George's Street, no. 122, a block by Maurice Tribich, 1976, has a carefully detailed replica façade of the Hanoverian original. North of it is a row of original houses with painted brickwork. No. 15 is the Palladian centrepiece of the street. Also of note in St George's Street are nos. 6–7, a chunky Edwardian Baroque design, and no. 25a, boarded up and awaiting redevelopment at the corner of Conduit Street. Though a not greatly distinguished brick and stucco palazzo of the 1840s, no. 25a nicely turns the corner and plays an important townscape role as the introduction to an area easily mauled by placeless modernist efforts. It should be position listed.

In Conduit and New Bond Streets are numerous examples of the rich and varied small-scale commercial architecture of the nineteenth century. Nos.

28–9 Conduit Street have post-Nash stucco fronts. The scale is diminutive, the details free and non-classical. South of Grafton Street in **New Bond Street** are nos. 165–9, Asprey's, with two-storey cast-iron columns and spandrels framing large sheets of plate-glass, a mid-Victorian front on buildings of the mid-Georgian period. South of Asprey's are nos. 169–74, a unified series of late neo-classic façades in stucco now painted in different colours with first-floor colonnades as an appropriate device seen foreshortened in this narrow portion of the street. When the street widens to the south, Cartier's, no. 176, presents a large, refined later Victorian stone façade to be appreciated frontally.

We return to Regent Street along Burlington Gardens, past the glass-roofed Burlington Arcade, 1815–19, by Samuel Ware. Then comes the former headquarters of London University, now the **Museum of Mankind**, an elaborate High Victorian classic design of 1869 by James Pennethorne. The skyline is well punctuated by the notables of philosophy and science. The sides and back of the building, in polychromatic brickwork with Italian Gothic arches, were apparently the losers in this skirmish of the 'Battle of the Styles'.

Burlington Gardens narrows into Vigo Street, and a Victorian stucco block closes the vista. South of it is the back entrance to Henry Holland's delightful Albany, of 1802 – two diminutive rows of bachelors' chambers about a covered walkway, entered from Piccadilly. Vigo Street leads on to the **Quadrant**, which follows the curve of Nash's approach to Piccadilly Circus.

Much of the rest of the original Regent Street was designed and built piecemeal by builders under Nash's general supervision. The Quadrant was crucial to the scheme; Nash designed it himself, invested his personal fortune in its construction, and when that did not suffice, persuaded his builder to take leases in lieu of payment. The result was an expanded version of the

St George's, Hanover Square, flanked by contemporary buildings, was designed as the gateway to Hanover Square. Introducing the ensemble from Conduit Street to the south are unlisted early and late Victorian buildings which merit protection. The corner block on the right, a Victorian palazzo occupying a key site, awaits demolition. Unprotected view

Crescent at Regent's Park, with continuous Roman Doric colonnaded porticos forming covered walkways on both sides of the street. The procession culminated in the **County Fire Office**, a copy of Inigo Jones' five-bay river frontage to Somerset House, facing Carlton House, a quarter-mile to the south, across a genuinely round Piccadilly Circus.

The destruction of the Quadrant began with the construction of Norman Shaw's **Piccadilly Hotel** in 1905. Its giant Genoese Baroque façade in the Quadrant's southern arm is the handsomest part of the present Quadrant; one only wishes Shaw had put it somewhere else. It was continued in a watered-down fashion on either side by Sir Reginald Blomfield. By 1923 all trace of Nash's work had disappeared. Trystan Edwards in *Good and Bad Manners in Architecture* wrote, prophetically, in 1924: 'The supposition that this cultural disaster was primarily due to the shortsightedness of men of commerce or of the general public would undoubtedly be pleasing to a professional self-respect, but unfortunately the evil was caused by a corruption of mind within the architectural citadel itself. ... It is the propagation of doctrines actually *ignoring* all the vital considerations of civic art which has been the real cause of the disaster of Regent's Street. That disaster is in its nature quite without parallel, and the heart grows sick at the contemplation of it.'

Of course the new Quadrant paid some deference to 'civic art'. Care was taken to frame the entrances to small adjacent streets and to Piccadilly with great rusticated arches, and a building by Ernest Newton vaguely like Nash's Fire Office was put up in its place; the new details were repeated on other buildings facing the 'circus'. Despite these palliatives, the sheet height and bulk of Shaw's and Blomfield's Quadrant shattered Nash's conception. His cornice line, barely as high as the capitals of the present giant columns, produced a graciously proportioned street where stone cliffs now wind their ponderous way to end in a striking contrast with **Piccadilly Circus**.

With the opening of Shaftesbury Avenue in 1885 the Circus became, in the words of Eros' sculptor Alfred Gilbert, 'a distorted isochromal triangle', and has been a graveyard of London plans ever since. (For details of some of them, and of the Circus' buildings, see Walk 3, page 54).

The final stretch of Nash's ceremonial way, and the one in which axial vistas played an important role, proceeds from Piccadilly Circus down **Lower Regent Street** to Waterloo Place and the site of Carlton House. A view of the route is obtained in front of the Fire Office's eastern arch. The Duke of York's Column, 1833, on the site of Carlton House is framed by Lower Regent Street; beyond it are the trees of St James's Park, then the Foreign Office, 1861, and completing the vista, just to the right of the Column, the Gothic silhouette of the **Victoria Tower** of the Houses of Parliament, designed by Charles Barry in 1835 and completed in 1860. From this vantage-point it may seem obvious that Barry, a neo-classic designer, intentionally completed Nash's great axis with a monument of national importance, but critical opinion generally maintains that Barry's placement of the towers of the Houses of Parliament was merely an attempt to create a 'spurious Gothic asymmetry'. It is a misconception of how a designer like Barry worked to imagine him scattering Gothic towers and spires about with the hope of achieving some vaguely conceived 'picturesqueness'. That, of course, is how a modernist would do it, and it is understandable that modernist criticism is unable to grasp the fact that for traditional architects the larger townscape context of a prominent building was the subject of careful study. For further evidence of Barry's conception of townscape, the view from the portico of the National Gallery to Big Ben should be examined (see Walk 3).

We proceed south along Lower Regent Street past stone-faced blocks in the abbreviated 'classical' style of the 1920s, or in the bare modernism of the 1950s. The *flèche* of the Houses of Parliament joins the Victoria Tower on the horizon. West of Charles II Street is St James's Square, and axially aligned

with it, along Nash's extension of Charles II Street to the east, is his stucco façade of the Theatre Royal, Haymarket, of 1821 – a six-columned Corinthian portico with a panel of delicate rosette-windows above the pediment.

The northern portion of **Waterloo Place** is symmetrically framed by two L-shaped ranges of 1920s blocks. They have arched, rusticated ground storeys, engaged giant order composite colonnades, and porticos with wreaths, garlands, and other classicizing paraphernalia. The whole design bears a resemblance to the original stucco blocks which it replaced, and to Carlton House to the south. The effect is decidedly superior to any of its contemporary neighbours.

The Guards Crimean Monument of 1859 dominates the centre of Waterloo Place above Pall Mall. Pall Mall East, cut through by Nash, gives a glimpse of the dome and portico of the National Gallery at Trafalgar Square. This is the only hint of the proximity of that central urban space, originally conceived by Nash, to his procession in Regent Street. Across Pall Mall on either side of Waterloo Place are two clubs planned as a pair: the **United Service Club**, a relatively restrained Nash design of 1827 to which Decimus Burton added a portico with paired Corinthian columns, a lush frieze and other signs of Victorian richness in 1842; and opposite on the west, an earlier Burton design, the **Athenaeum** of 1829. The building has a modest Greek Doric entrance portico and a Grecian frieze recalling the Parthenon, but the window surrounds with bracketed flat entablatures at the heads, the absence of colonnades and pilasters, and the block-like character of the whole mark

The Victoria Tower of the Houses of Parliament, a neo-Gothic monument in the neo-classical frame of Lower Regent Street, dominates the view as one moves south from Piccadilly Circus

the beginning of the astylar phase of later neo-classicism which rejected Greek forms and took instead the palazzi of the Italian Renaissance as inspiration. Adjacent to the west in Pall Mall are two fully-developed Renaissance designs by Charles Barry which together with the Athenaeum form an irresistible ensemble. The **Travellers' Club** of 1829 and the **Reform Club** of 1837 set the style for three decades of Victorian residential and commercial architecture. The façades have plain wall surfaces, quoins at the corners, pedimented windows, and projecting cornices. The Reform Club, modelled on the Palazzo Farnese, is the larger and stronger of the two, with a particularly rich cornice.

Benjamin Wyatt's Duke of York's column and Nash's broad **Duke of York Steps**, flanked by Carlton House Terrace, were the site of Carlton House, begun for George III by Henry Holland in 1783. Despite the vast planning scheme based on its position, Carlton House was pulled down in 1827 when the Regent, then George IV, moved his residence to Nash's new Buckingham Palace. The destruction of Carlton House may have seemed wanton and extravagant, but Nash was surely right in opening a grand entrance to the park here. East of the column, closing the view along the back of Carlton House Terrace, is the concrete grid of the British Council, built on the site of Nash's attractive Carlton Mews, pulled down by the Crown Estates' Commissioners in 1969.

Looking back to Piccadilly Circus, and recalling the walk from Regent's Park, one may wonder at the erasure, less than a century after its completion, of so much of London's most ambitious scheme. In the late nineteenth century, and well into the twentieth, Nash's stucco architecture seems to have been despised on all sides: by classicists for its theatricality and 'slovenly' details, by Gothicists for its classicism, by eclectics for its

Decimus Burton's Athenaeum in Waterloo Place and Charles Barry's Travellers' and Reform Clubs show the transition from the Grecian to the neo-Renaissance style which occurred about 1830

*Nash's Theatre Royal, Haymarket,
closes the view from Charles II Street*

uniformity, and by techno-fetishists for its 'dishonesty'. The crux of the
problem was the nearly exclusive concern of architectural critics with the
moral and ideological implications of technological processes, materials and
of stylistic detail, resulting in the proverbial blindness of twentieth-century
architects to the larger perception of townscape. This is what prompted
Trystan Edwards to write in 1924: 'Often I lie awake at night and imagine
that I can hear an odious grating sound, and that I can see a still more odious
sight of ugly little teeth, crooked, self-righteous little teeth – the Ruskinian
rats are gnawing away at masterpiece after masterpiece of our national civic
art.'

In another sense, Nash's Regent Street was the victim of its own success. It
provided the north–south link essential for this part of London; its
alignment stitched together Soho, Mayfair and St James along a broad and
successful commercial thoroughfare connected with residential districts to
the north. The street had great potential for further exploitation, and with
the rise of twentieth-century mass shopping, the original small-scale
accommodation was doomed by the Crown Estates' bookkeepers as well as
by 'Ruskinian rats'.

Carlton House Terrace, 1827–9, is Nash's heroic backdrop to St James's
Park. Identical blocks on either side of the Duke of York's steps accompany
the ceremonial procession of the Mall for nearly 1300 feet of its length with
extended giant order Corinthian colonnades supporting plain, balustraded
entablatures which continue across the faces of high end pavilions. The
grand design is brought down to eye level by the lines of stout, cast-iron
Doric columns which frame segmental arches and panels of vermiculated
rustication on the façades of the terraces' projecting bases.

The Mall is reputed to have been laid out by the Parisian landscape
designer Le Nôtre for King Charles II. Nash extended the avenue to George
IV's Buckingham Palace. The Mall's entrance from Trafalgar Square to the
east is marked by Sir Aston Webb's Admiralty Arch, 1910. Webb's Victoria
Memorial, 1911, and refronted Buckingham Palace, 1912, terminate the vista

164243

Although his original Gothic design failed to win the competition for a new Foreign and Colonial Office in 1856, G. G. Scott persuaded the Prime Minister, Lord Palmerston, to let him build the project. Palmerston agreed, but demanded a classical design. Scott, a convinced Gothicist, finally purchased a set of classical copy-books, braced himself with quinine and sea air, and produced the design of the present building in 1861. He took elements from the Venetian Renaissance, but managed to slip in Gothic polychromatic decoration where he could, across the entablatures, on string courses, and as panels below the windows

to the west. **St James's Park**, originally marshland, was acquired by Henry VII from the Abbot of Westminster and used as a deer park. It was laid out in a formal manner for Charles II, with a straight canal, 'the long water', as its central feature. Nash redesigned the park in its present picturesque form in 1828 and reshaped the canal into a meandering lake which skilfully focuses views along its length towards the Horse Guards Palace to the east. Nash's designs of Regent's and St James's Parks, which reflect his years of partnership with Humphry Repton, are probably the most outstanding part of his townplanning scheme, and are certainly the most generally appreciated and enjoyed. His career ended abruptly with his dismissal as architect of Buckingham Palace in 1830. A parliamentary investigation into the palace's spiralling costs revealed his involvement in financial irregularities. Publicly disgraced, John Nash died in 1835.

The **Horse Guards Parade** east of St James's Park is bounded by a U-shaped group made up of the backs and extensions of government buildings in Whitehall. On the north, faced with brown aggregate and covered in ivy, like a ruin from Hadrian's time, is the Admiralty's **Citadel**, a Second World War bunker. Next to it is the bright red-brick and stone late Victorian Baroque **Admiralty** by Leeming and Leeming, with a pair of ribbed green copper pavilion domes. The Admiralty's other domes have been skilfully placed in response to views from Trafalgar Square. On the east, at the centre, is William Kent's **Horse Guards**, completed by Vardy in 1760, surmounted by an octagonal Baroque-scrolled lantern dome and cupola which, together with the stone cupolas of the Ministry of Defence in Whitehall, 1907, by William Young, and the black pavilion roofs of the Whitehall Club, 1875, by Archer and Green, form a remarkable skyline ensemble, best seen from the bridge across the lake in St James's Park. This is one of the six central London views the GLC would like to see preserved.

South of the parade is Kent's **Old Treasury**, the centre portion of a Palladian design never completed. It has, like the Horse Guards, rustication all the way up, and blank arches around the windows. There is also an engaged portico at first storey level; next are the backs of nos. 10 and 11 Downing Street, overshadowed by George Gilbert Scott's **Foreign Office**. The façade in Whitehall displays tiers of arches flanked by sculpture, the sides are plainer, while the back at St James's Park is a big, free, genuinely picturesque composition. The design further develops neo-classic pictur-esqueness, based upon simple axiality and pure geometry, into a dynamic composition which, appropriate to its position, has a unity when seen from a distance, while accompanying the moving viewer nearby with an evolving variety of forms. From the north there is a squat angle tower, a return corner, then, precisely aligned on the Piccadilly Circus–Victoria Tower axis, a soaring corner tower with a lower wing attached, sweeping round to meet a six-bay projection that recalls the Whitehall façade. Scott credited the bold conception to one of his draughtsmen, Matthew Digby Wyatt.

South of the Foreign Office is the back of the late Victorian **Government Offices**. Looming over the park on the south-west is the monstrous new **Home Office** by Basil Spence and Fitzroy Robinson and Partners. Great George Street presents a view east to Parliament Square, Big Ben and the Houses of Parliament. For details of these, see Walks 3 and 5.

Walk 5 begins at the Houses of Parliament.

Walk 3   Piccadilly Circus to Parliament Square

London's world-famous public urban spaces, Piccadilly Circus, Leicester Square and Trafalgar Square, centres of mass entertainment and public assembly, are clustered within a few hundred yards of each other in the heart of the capital, yet lack the essential visual relation and sense of orientation among them which one normally finds in similar circumstances in continental cities. Some visitors actually have difficulty in finding Leicester Square from either of the neighbouring spaces. John Nash, who planned both Piccadilly Circus and Trafalgar Square, tried to connect them but failed, and planners, with a few notable exceptions, have been stumbling in the area ever since. On the other hand, the link between Trafalgar Square and Parliament Square is one of the finest achievements of traditional English townplanning.

Piccadilly Circus became a centre of London night-life in the 1870s. Theatres, music halls, restaurants and cafés, notably Archer and Green's luxuriant High Victorian Café Royal, 1872, rebuilt 1928, and Frank and Thomas Verity's handsomely decorated Criterion Theatre, 1874–84, were joined in 1885 by the stucco–Renaissance London Pavilion, built with the opening of Shaftesbury Avenue. The introduction of the avenue transformed Nash's Circus into an awkward space, but Alfred Gilbert's Eros fountain, 1893, a memorial to the philanthropist Lord Shaftesbury, provided an effective visual focus. The destruction of the original Quadrant and the surviving parts of the Circus after the First World War, and the insertion of over-scaled pomposities of 1920s 'classicism' threw a shadow over the smaller-scaled 'pleasing confusion' of the Victorian buildings to the east. Their subsequent concealment behind advertising hoardings marked the disappearance of café society and the replacement of theatre and variety by canned entertainments, accelerating the architectural and physical decline of the area. This, combined with master plans to double the volume of traffic through the Circus made it the obvious target for speculative acquisition and comprehensive redevelopment.

The present shabbiness of Piccadilly Circus is the result of the proposal and rejection of a remarkable series of plans, eight in all, over the last twenty years, beginning with a traffic scheme of the London County Council in 1958 and culminating in a design produced in 1972 by a star-studded cast of developers' architects. The plan was truly awe-inspiring – on a *tabula rasa* site only Eros survived, raised on a deck above a vast interchange surrounded by gigantic office and hotel blocks sited according to the principles of what Americans call 'railroad-wreck planning'.

The scheme had the strong support of Westminster's planners. In a *quid pro quo* arrangement the planners of the GLC left Piccadilly Circus entirely in the hands of Westminster, while they busied themselves, without Westminster's interference, in the planning of Covent Garden, with equally disastrous results. Well-organized public opposition crushed both plans, effectively ending comprehensive redevelopment schemes for this part of London. Some sites around the Circus continue to decay, others are being redeveloped piecemeal. Thomas Verity's listed extension to the Criterion, no. 223, with elegant banqueting rooms, is to be demolished, along with the adjoining Edwardian group turning into Haymarket, while small Victorian buildings facing the Circus on the north have already come down, virtually overnight. Unannounced demolition can take place because most of Piccadilly Circus is not a Conservation Area.

A detail from the 'Cinzano' building facing the Circus. Beneath the blandishments of late-twentieth-century advertising lie Victorian decorative motifs. The classicists' favourite plant form, the acanthus, here lushly enfolds a grinning satyr

So far no steps have been taken to coordinate a townscape policy for the area. All the frontages in Shaftesbury Avenue north of the Circus, comprising a variety of late Victorian buildings, including the pink, phantasmagoric Trocadero, have been excluded from the recently expanded Soho Conservation Area. Here, as in Coventry Street east of the Circus, the disdain of Westminster Council's 'classicists' for ornate Victoriana coincides nicely with plans for speculative redevelopment and road widening.

Coventry and **New Coventry Streets** lead to Leicester Square. The crossing of Whitcomb Street, a medieval alignment from Charing Cross, is marked by a large-scale group – on the south-west, the curved Second Empire façade, recently cleaned, surmounted by a pavilion roof, identifies Leicester Square from Charing Cross Road to the east; on the south-east Fanum House (the Automobile Association) by Andrew Marther, 1923, is a steel-framed block with chamfered corners, giant Corinthian columns set in the concave recesses of three-storey glass and bronze enamelled bays, a more gracious effect than the contemporary heavy stone fronts in Regent Street; on the north-east, the rounded corners and illuminated print-out of the Swiss Centre, 1961–8, by Davis du R. Aberdeen, are devices of modern townscape well used here. North of the Swiss Centre closing the view in Leicester Street is Frank Verity's St John's Hospital, 1897.

Leicester Square was laid out south of the Earl of Leicester's house in 1670. The square remained isolated from main roads and virtually hidden until New Coventry and Cranbourn streets were cut through in 1843. *Punch* then speculated about the 'native tribes who might still abide from the centuries the square has remained undisturbed' which the 'expedition to the interior of Leicester Square' might encounter. Buildings around the squares subsequently joined those in Piccadilly Circus as centres of entertainment. The mid-Victorian Alhambra, replaced by the black, functionalist Odeon in

A view of Piccadilly Circus as it appeared in 1890. The buildings seen here all still exist, though obscured by advertising hoardings. The GLC's initiative in cleaning and repairing the façades of the London Pavilion should be followed elsewhere. Unfortunately, Westminster Council seems to prefer demolition and more honky-tonk

1937, and Thomas Verity's Empire, 1882, now also a cinema, were the most prominent. Next to the Empire is the remarkable Victorian Rococo Queen's House of 1897.

For decades after the new streets opened the square, it remained covered in weeds owing to disagreements among its various owners. Finally in 1874 the square was purchased, landscaped, besculptured, and donated to the public by the fraudulent tycoon and MP, Baron Grant. His fictitious financial empire collapsed soon after, eighty-nine legal actions were brought against him, and his creditors were left holding the bag for the 'barren grant'. Some of his unlucky investors may have ruefully contemplated the inscription on Shakespeare's statue at the centre of the square – 'there is no darkness but ignorance'.

Credit for the pleasant and well-executed pedestrianization of Leicester Square belongs to the GLC. The plan encountered stiff opposition and delaying tactics from Westminster Council, who feared the new landscaping would become a 'vandalized tourist camp', attracting the 'undesirable elements' already drawn to the area by their planning of Piccadilly Circus.

Irving Street, leading to Charing Cross Road, has an attractive mixture of Victorian red-brick and stucco frontages, but is not part of the Conservation Area, since, like other streets south of Leicester Square, it is being 'safeguarded' as a possible route for the GLC traffic planners' 'Orange Street Connector'. Charing Cross Road was cut through in 1887, skirting the back of the National Gallery and opening views to James Gibbs' **St Martin-in-the-Fields**, 1726. Gibbs' six-columned Corinthian portico resembles Nicholas Hawksmoor's design of 1716 at St George's, Bloomsbury, and John James' west front at Hanover Square (Walks 1 and 2). The steeple was originally intended as the focus of framed views from St Martin's Lane to the north. The soaring height also played a dominant role on the skyline seen from the Thames, reflecting St Martin's importance as the parish church of the Royal Family.

The church and its vestry hall to the north flank a view along St Martin's Mews to the west façade of Nash's 'pepper pots'. The centre portion of this elevation was occupied by Witherden Young's Lowther Arcade, 1831, replaced in 1903 by MacVicar Anderson's listed Coutts' Bank. When Anderson made a measured drawing out of respect for the old Arcade before its demolition he could hardly have imagined that a replica of Young's façade would replace his own seventy-five years later. Frederick Gibberd is the architect for the new Coutts' Bank. St Martin-in-the-Fields and the 'pepper pots' are still being 'safeguarded' as sites for the Orange Street Connector – a tribute to the astonishing tenacity of the GLC traffic planners.

The portico of St Martin's provides an introductory view of **Trafalgar Square** dominated by Nelson's Column, with the Admiralty's green copper dome prominent on the skyline. In the foreground is an equestrian statue of George IV, under whose aegis the square was first conceived by John Nash in 1812. He sketched out the square's present position and size in about 1820.

Trafalgar Square is London's 'front parlour'; unlike the residential squares it was intended from the start as a public space. Its position at the intersection of Whitehall and the Strand reflects the great bend in the Thames nearby, and incorporates Charing Cross, the medieval turning-point of the corridor built up between Westminster Abbey and St Paul's Cathedral. The square links Westminster to the City – the centres of government and finance; it also marks the transition between the commercial district of the Strand and aristocratic St James and the Royal Parks to the west. Small businesses and working-class areas in Soho and Covent Garden to the north face the Civil Service and Parliament down Whitehall to the south. Because of its central position Trafalgar Square has been the traditional focus of political demonstrations.

The area had been a Royal Mews and menagerie since the fourteenth century; humble residences and well-known pubs later clustered nearby.

These were cleared away between 1826 and 1830, with some protest. The Royal Stables designed by William Kent remained on the site now occupied by the **National Gallery** until 1835. The stables first quartered the Horse Guards' horses; later, in the 1820s, they were used for public exhibitions of the mechanical arts. William Wilkins' National Gallery was completed in 1838. Parliament compelled Wilkins to reuse parts of the colonnade of Carlton House, pulled down in 1827. The scale of the dominant feature of the National Gallery's façade was thus determined by the relatively small columns originally designed by Henry Holland for a much more modest site, and this may explain the weakness of Wilkins' design in relation to the square.

As we approach the gallery's entrance portico along from St Martin's, the Victoria Tower of the Houses of Parliament, and then the *flèche* appear down the corridor of Whitehall. Framed by the columns of the gallery's portico on the axis of the square, the view focuses, with considerable effect, upon the clock tower of the Houses of Parliament, Big Ben, completed to Charles Barry's design in 1858. The tower's position as seen from here, appearing just to the left of William Railton's axially placed **Nelson's Column**, put up in 1839, was almost certainly intended by Barry. The National Gallery portico, the Column, the square and the clock tower of Parliament are all national monuments of the first importance. Barry, a neo-classicist, could hardly have ignored their visual connections. Even if he had not taken the National Gallery view into account in the original design of 1835, now lost, he could not have missed it when he designed the terrace in front of the National Gallery and laid out the square symmetrically about this axis in 1840.

Barry's fountains and their large pools were partly inspired by the government's desire to break up the unruly mobs which might gather here, and perhaps to dampen protesters' ire. Following the mass meeting of the Chartist Movement in 1848, demonstrations were banned from the square until 1892. Attempts to hold socialist rallies here in 1886 were harshly turned back by troops and police.

The gallery's portico presents a vantage-point for observing the character of the square and the buildings around it. Nelson's Column, surmounted by a Corinthian capital cast from the bronze of captured French cannon, and by the figure of Lord Nelson, equals the height of an eighteen-storey building. The flanking monumental lions were completed by Edwin Landseer in 1867. Barry's fountains were modernized by Edwin Lutyens in 1939. The buildings around the square vary in height and style, but are nearly all faced in Bath or Portland stone, and often repeat classical themes of string-courses, cornices, and balustrades. Their skylines are well punctuated by pavilion roofs, chimneys and spires. Many of the buildings follow street intersections with simple curves.

South of St Martin's on the east side of the square is Herbert Baker's **South Africa House**, 1935, a stripped-down classical effort which matches the (excessive) height of Grand Buildings next to it and answers the large curve of its façade with a small rounded portico at the entrance to the Strand. The rounded forms of **Grand Buildings**, 1878, and **Trafalgar Buildings**, 1881, south-west of it, designed by the Francis Brothers, were built astride the site of the Jacobean Northumberland House, pulled down when Northumberland Avenue was cut through to the Embankment in 1874. The destruction of Northumberland House provoked strong protests from London's early preservationists. The buildings replacing it, designed in the crude, vital and heavily eclectic English version of the Second Empire style, were denounced from the start. Grand and Trafalgar Buildings have continued to inspire the unjustified scorn of art historians for having 'motifs from many styles spread across their façades'. Reflecting Trafalgar Buildings' curve across Whitehall is the **Royal Bank of Scotland** of 1885. The classical style and rounded corner are in turn repeated across the entrance to the Mall by Reginald Blomfield's **Uganda House** of 1915. The well-sited late Victorian 'wrenaissance' dome of the **Admiralty** rises at the end of Spring Gardens' narrow corridor, framed between the two curved façades north of it. **Canada House**, facing the square on the west, is a much altered version of the building designed in 1827 by Robert Smirke, with elegantly austere Doric porticos surviving on the north and south.

Trafalgar Square as a whole lacks the homogeneity and the sense of enclosure found in Italian piazzas. Its sloping site, the varied height and character of its buildings, and the entrance into it at various angles of no less than eight main roads all give the square a somewhat disjointed quality.

The square's shortcomings compared with the qualities of Mediterranean urban spaces led Westminster Council's townscape analysts to the alarming conclusion that Trafalgar Square was 'leaking space', most seriously around Grand and Trafalgar Buildings. Speculative developers conveniently had produced a plan to replace Grand and Trafalgar Buildings and to repair the leak. A remarkable exhibition of the scheme was held in the foyer of the National Gallery in October 1974. There was an enchanting scale model of the improved square, with the delicious miniature cars and buses which planning committees find so irresistible. There was also a questionnaire for the public which bore the unctious traces of the public relations man's art – its begged questions precluded any negative responses: 'Which of the improvements which the proposals will bring do you consider most important – improved working conditions, improved view down Whitehall . . .' etc.

The design was the work of R. Seifert and Partners, and T.P. Bennett and Son, with William Whitfield as coordinating architect. The proposed buildings generally followed the height and volume of the existing ones, but not their skylines, and the simple convexity of Trafalgar Buildings' curved façade, which leads the eye so well down Whitehall to the spires of Westminster, was to be replaced by a bumpy, concave arrangement, apparently intended to impede the 'leaking space'.

Trafalgar Square seen from the National Gallery portico. The principal buildings around the square from left to right are Africa House, Grand Buildings, Trafalgar Buildings, the Royal Bank of Scotland and Uganda House. The view down Whitehall is dominated by Big Ben, and the shorter corridor of Spring Gardens is marked by a corner tower of the Admiralty

The *Architects' Journal* denounced the scheme as 'an exercise in crude gigantism and a shameful waste of resources'. It also deplored the planned 700% increase in rents and the driving-out from central London of 180 flourishing small businesses. On the other hand the Victorian Society saw no reason for defending the old buildings and the Royal Fine Arts Commission, composed largely of eminent architects, also found them of no architectural value, agreed with the townscape analysts, and endorsed the redevelopment. One prominent insider dismissed this endorsement as 'a case of dog not eating dog'.

A counter-exhibition was held on the steps of St Martin-in-the-Fields and 13,000 signatures opposing the scheme were presented at Westminster City Hall. The deputation was not well received, and Westminster's approval of the plan seemed likely. But in the end the issue was decided, not by mass demonstrations, arm-twisting, or a lengthy and expensive public inquiry, the results of which would have disappeared for months, or years, down the anonymous corridors of the DOE. Instead, the Trafalgar Square Association of tenants and those concerned about the square made a direct appeal to the members of Westminster Council. Rather than heaping abuse upon the politicians, the Association wisely decided to use more civilized kinds of persuasion. The councillors were shown around the buildings, which they had not visited before, and then, following refreshments, they were reminded that the old buildings were sound and usable, needing only the repairs which the owners had withheld for some years. The architectural quality of the buildings was emphasized. The defenders of Grand and Trafalgar Buildings breathed a secret sigh of relief that no one had brought up the Victorian comments which had greeted their construction a century before: 'staring monstrosities', 'money without culture', 'the most vulgar corner in London', and the Swiss art historian Jacob Burkhardt's description of Grand Buildings, 'an oval stone belly'.

Westminster's Chief Architect, Joe Hirsch, sensibly agreed with the tenants that the buildings formed a part of the 'historic backcloth to the square'. Sir James Richards, Sir John Betjeman and Lord Gibson, then chairman of the Arts Council, lent the weight of their support to the Association's case. In April 1975, Westminster Council refused planning permission for the proposed scheme. The Battle of Trafalgar Square was won. Land Securities, owners of Grand Buildings, gracefully accepted defeat and quickly cleaned and repaired their building. The refurbishment of Trafalgar Buildings has followed.

The square and its setting seen from ground level. The banner on Grand Buildings at the left announcing that 'London belongs to the people' was displayed during the 'Battle of Trafalgar Square'

William Wilkins' National Gallery has often been disparaged for its weakness in relation to Trafalgar Square, but its dome does provide an effective focal point for views up Whitehall. The GLC High Building Policy is pledged to protect this vista

Because of the hazardous traffic, the best approach to Charing Cross and Whitehall is along the west side of the square. Opposite the severe neo-classic south portico of Smirke's Canada House is the jeweller's delicacy of the National Westminster Bank by F.W. Porter, of 1871, faced in Portland stone and polished granite. To the west, further on, the curved front of Sir Aston Webb's ponderous Admiralty Arch marks the entrance to the Mall, Buckingham Palace and the Royal Parks.

Charing Cross was a memorial put up by Edward I to his Queen Eleanor in 1290 and pulled down by Cromwell's iconoclastic Parliament in 1647. The figure of Charles I, placed here in 1675, faces towards Parliament and toward the site of his execution at its hands, in front of Inigo Jones' Banqueting House.

The statue marks the beginning of **Whitehall**, a slightly meandering alignment of varying width partially occupied by private residences and lodging houses until the nineteenth century, and now largely taken up by a mixture of Georgian, Victorian and Edwardian buildings housing the 'tangled nuclei of power' and leading to their traditional centre at the Palace of Westminster opposite Westminster Abbey.

The subtle and complex magnetism of the various activities of government – attracting and repelling one another, shifting claims and alliances, marking out hierarchies, boundaries, and barriers – has operated, in typical London fashion, over centuries without the benefit of a unified formal plan. The system of pragmatic accommodation and the resultant ambiguity of relationships and the fluidity of physical forms is characteristic of the British system of government and its constitution, and recalls, by way of contrast, the unambiguous relation of the branches of the American government, defined with concise logic in the constitution, and expressed with fixed visual clarity in the plan of Washington, DC.

Whitehall has seen a good deal of change in the position of important functions and the disappearance and replacement of most of its buildings. The Crown and the Law left the area to Parliament and the expanding Civil Service, with only the Church remaining on its ancient site at Westminster Abbey. Despite this, the architects who built up the street have shown the particular English gift of making their buildings appear more or less as if they had always been there, an achievement even more remarkable in view of the innovative role many of them played in the history of English architecture.

There are fine views from in front of the **Ministry of Defence** (War Office), on the east side of Whitehall, back to the dome of the National Gallery, and down to the three spires of the Houses of Parliament which fill the skyline. The Ministry of Defence, designed by William Young in 1898 and completed after his death by his son, is one of Whitehall's most effective townscape pieces. The Baroque domes above its corner towers contribute to some of London's finest vistas – from Trafalgar and Parliament Squares, and from St James's Park. The scale of Young's colonnade is attuned to that of the Banqueting House to the south, and repeats its capitals, while its muscular Victorian Baroque form maintains its own character.

William Kent's **Horse Guards** faces the Ministry of Defence. The Horse Guards were first housed on this site in 1680 when Charles II decided he would do well to station troops near his residence in Whitehall Palace. Kent's design of 1745 was completed after his death by John Vardy in 1760. The Horse Guards' lively composition is distinctly non-Palladian. The arch-framed view to St James's Park reminds us that the building's picturesque massing was intended as a gateway to the landscape. The rest of the buildings on this side of Whitehall simply present their backs to the park. South of the Horse Guards, is Henry Holland's entrance to **Dover House**, 1787, now the Scottish Office. It has a delicate, scholarly Ionic portico flanked by free-standing columns on either side, each with its own projecting bit of entablature, repeating a feature of the Banqueting House opposite. Holland's elegant little design, which brought French Revolutionary neo-classicism to London, has been accused of harbouring the seeds of modernism.

Inigo Jones' **Banqueting House** was the major début of the Italian Renaissance style in London. The two-storey Palladian façade belies the magnificent double-cube hall within. It was built in 1619 as the first stage in Inigo's plan for James I's new Royal Palace. According to one version, it occupied the north-east corner of a projected U-shaped composition opening to the Thames. The southern twin of the Banqueting House would have occupied the present site of Richmond Terrace, one hundred yards to the south. The old Whitehall Palace which Inigo's scheme was to replace had been built up in a haphazard fashion by Henry VIII on land seized from Cardinal Wolsey, Archbishop of York, in 1529. The original Royal Palace next to Westminster Abbey, which Henry VIII had abandoned for this site, was taken over by Parliament. In the 1680s Christopher Wren added some long brick ranges to Whitehall Palace for Charles II. In 1698 the entire complex burnt down, except the Banqueting House, which was saved by strenuous efforts. Wren then produced a plan incorporating the Banqueting House as the centrepiece of a vast Baroque palace, linking the Thames to St James's Park, but the scheme was not carried out. The royal residence shifted to St James's Palace and never returned to Whitehall. The site of Whitehall Palace was taken over by the Privy Gardens, and then the Civil Service. As their role became increasingly ceremonial, British monarchs retired to Buckingham Palace, in the picturesque grandeur of the Royal Parks.

The exercise of political power in Britain now focuses upon the 'village centre' of Whitehall – the small buildings of the **Cabinet Office** and the prime minister's residence and offices at **10 Downing Street**, behind their unassuming early Georgian façades. Here a few hundred 'villagers' within walking distance of each other formulate the policies which Parliament later debates down the road, and which armies of civil servants then administer from their imposing blocks nearby.

The façade of the present Cabinet Office (formerly the Treasury) was designed by Charles Barry in 1845, reusing the Corinthian colonnade and floral frieze from Soane's Board of Trade built here in 1827 and dismantled in 1844. Until 1964, when the building was gutted and rebuilt within, parts of Henry VIII's Whitehall Palace, and even traces of a structure from the ninth century were entwined in the labyrinth of rooms which lay behind the present front. The façades' repeated projected entablatures recall the similar feature at Dover House to the north. The charm of that design lies in its ability to be contemplated by the mind's eye as a precise combination of shapes and volumes. The Soane/Barry Cabinet Office is much more an urbanistic work. The blocks of entablature, surmounted by a double tier of balustrades and a line of pinnacles, have been conceived in perspective for the passer-by, and are particularly effective because of the building's splayed position in relation to its neighbours.

Opposite the Cabinet Office is **Gwydyr House**, the Welsh Office, built as a private residence in 1772 shortly before the Building Act standardized the proportions of Georgian façades. South of it is the new **Ministry of Defence** building, a work which seems to have been pinned down between the opposing fronts of modernism and classicism. It was based on a 1913 design by Vincent Harris, and finally completed in 1959. **Richmond Terrace** to the south is a well-proportioned and finely detailed neo-classic design of 1822. Its façade badly needs maintenance by its owners – the Department of the Environment.

George Gilbert Scott's **Foreign Office** opposite, completed in 1873, reflects the exuberant High Victorian taste for variety and expanse. A classical design by a Gothic Revival architect, the Whitehall façade performs, in nineteenth-century imperial terms, the function of a Gothic cathedral's west front: the sculptured panels between the lower arches represent the principal fields of human endeavour, and the earth's geographical divisions; the corresponding plaques in the tier of arches above present the heroes of the nation who respectively promoted or conquered them. At the top is the seated figure of Britannia, with the face of Queen Victoria.

Opposite the Foreign Office in the middle of Whitehall/Parliament Street is Edwin Lutyens' stark, carefully proportioned war memorial of 1919, the **Cenotaph**. Across King Charles Street, south of the Foreign Office, is J.M. Brydon's **Government Offices**, now the Treasury, of 1898 – an example of the late Victorian Baroque, more massive and less intricate than its neighbour to the north. Facing them across Parliament Street are privately built Georgian and Victorian structures now owned by the government. Particularly noteworthy are no. 54, a red-brick Baroque design of 1898; no. 47, Charles Parnell's 'florid Italianate' **Whitehall Club**, of 1864, with a fine big cornice and heavy swags on the frieze below; and nos. 43 and 44, houses of the mid-eighteenth century. The townscape importance of the east side of Parliament Street rivals that of the more prestigious blocks opposite, particularly in relation to the approach to the Houses of Parliament. Although Leslie Martin's scheme to demolish the southern part of Whitehall has been dropped, and plans for a new Parliamentary office block in Bridge Street have been shelved, the Victorian Society warns of government intentions eventually to demolish the east side of Parliament Street and to construct there a series of blocks to house more civil servants. The DOE's lack of enthusiasm for the buildings now in their care, reflected by minimal maintenance, lends weight to the warning.

Parliament Square, cleared in 1850, is Charles Barry's simple foreground to the magnificent silhouette of the Houses of Parliament on the east and to Westminster Abbey on the south. Bounding the square on the north is the main façade of the Government Offices, a final effusion of the Imperial Baroque, with powerful towers flanking the entrance. On the west are Alfred Waterhouse's Institute of Chartered Surveyors, 1898, and the Edwardian neo-Gothic Middlesex Guildhall. The square was enlarged, and its paving and statuary rearranged by Grey Wornum in 1951. Among the figures on the north and west sides are a massive Sir Winston Churchill, Field Marshal Smuts leaning off his pedestal, Disraeli, and a sartorially impeccable Lord Palmerston, George Gilbert Scott's determined classical opponent in the 'Battle of the Styles'. On the west is the tall, rumpled figure of Abraham Lincoln.

The site of **Westminster Abbey** was once an island between two branches of the River Tyburn, which meandered through the marshy monastic lands to the north-west. Edward the Confessor replaced tenth-century monastic buildings with a new monastery and church consecrated just before his death in 1065. His church in the Norman style was demolished by Henry III and a structure in the up-to-date French Gothic style was begun in its place in 1245. Construction of the half-finished nave was halted in 1269, and begun again in a faithful reproduction of the earlier style by the master mason Henry Yevele in 1375. Christopher Wren recommended extensive restoration and improvements in 1713, including the addition of a spire over the crossing and Gothic towers at the west front. These were designed by

Inigo Jones' Banqueting House and the Edwardian Baroque Ministry of Defence (old War Office) represent the beginning and end of the classical tradition in English architecture. Together with Dover House and the old Treasury (Cabinet Office) opposite, they form a carefully considered sequential composition developed over three centuries, rich in the mutual reference of form and detail

Parliament Street's arresting mixture of Georgian-to-mid-Victorian balustrades and repeated cornices combined with more elaborate later Victorian roofscapes all stand under the threat of government-encouraged decay.
Unprotected view

Nicholas Hawksmoor in 1734 and were completed after his death by his friend John James in 1745. James also added the square tower to St Margaret's, north of the Abbey, in 1737. In 1875 extensive restoration work was begun by George Gilbert Scott; much of the Abbey's exterior was refaced and the thirteenth-century north transept was virtually rebuilt in a manner which drew sharp criticism from preservationists.

From the time of the last Saxon kings, royalty maintained a close connection with the monastery and church at Westminster. William the Conqueror and most subsequent British monarchs were crowned here. They preferred the monkish company of the Benedictines to that of City merchants and bankers, and resided within the monastic sanctuary east of the Abbey, where the Houses of Parliament now stand, from the time of Edward the Confessor until Henry VIII moved the Royal Palace to Whitehall in 1529. Parliament, which had until then assembled in the Abbey chapter house, soon took over the vacated palace. **Westminster Hall**, first built by William Rufus in 1099, and given its astounding hammer-beam roof in 1401, designed by the master carpenter Hugh Herland, and the Jewel Tower of 1366 opposite Old Palace Yard are surviving parts of the royal complex.

After fire destroyed the old Houses of Parliament in 1834, only Westminster Hall and the Law Courts by Kent and Soane next to it remained. The Courts were pulled down in 1882 when the lawyers were sent off to the Strand; the Hall was incorporated in the new **Palace of Westminster** designed by Charles Barry and Augustus Pugin, the winners in the 1835 competition which specified the Gothic or Elizabethan style, marking official acceptance of the growing Gothic Revival.

Barry the neo-classicist and Pugin the Gothicist worked together in the harmony of mutual respect, and the building they produced – its romanticism tempered by logic – is perhaps the finest monument of English nineteenth-century architecture. The efficient, symmetrical neo-classic plan, the ingenious structural system, and the massing of the silhouette are Barry's work; the breathtaking Gothic detail inside and out is Pugin's.

For Pugin, the Gothic Revival was not just a matter of style, it was a religious and moral conviction. The ecclesiastical associations of Gothic forms, the mystical power of the geometry which lay behind them, and the redemptive force of creative Gothic craftsmanship, freeing workmen from enslavement to the mechanical repetition of alien classical detail, were all to come together in a 'Palace of History and Art', where legislators would be uplifted and true British art would be nurtured. His heroic efforts were ill-rewarded; the Parliamentary Commissioners hounded him incessantly, decried his efforts, and halved his salary. 'Still', he said near the end of his life, 'I think I have done some good.' He died insane at forty.

Facing the Houses of Parliament on the north, across the **New Palace Yard**, a major urban space of the fifteenth century, where a medieval fountain was unearthed during the installation of the Members' underground car park, is a block of Victorian buildings in private use. The development of the government precinct and its physical structure suggest that here size does not necessarily indicate power, nor is proximity a sign of functional connection. Some uses remain as buffers between potential antagonists, others block inappropriate expansion. Thus a collection of privately constructed commercial structures has been allowed to remain on the site nearest the seat of Parliamentary power, and indeed to overshadow it. The rules of Whitehall's urban geographical game of chess, along with restrictions on government spending, have so far prevented the construction here of a vast parliamentary office complex, an arrangement one may hope continues.

Walk 5 begins at the Houses of Parliament.

Charles Barry's design of Parliament Square opened the view to Westminster Hall and the stunning skyline of his Houses of Parliament. Buildings in excess of twelve storeys across the Thames will intrude upon this view, but the GLC High Building Policy (GLDP 1976) sees no reason to restrict building heights there. Unprotected view

Walk 4 Charing Cross to St Paul's Cathedral

The Strand and Fleet Street follow the approximate line of an old road leading from the Roman city to the west. In late Saxon times it was London's major suburban route, connecting the medieval walled city with the turning, or Charing, to the royal and monastic complex at Westminster. By the thirteenth century the street had been built up on either side with more or less continuous ribbon development. Those who had special status under the feudal system, and thus did not require or were not allowed the privileges and protection granted city-dwellers by royal charter, took up positions outside the walls. Among those who built up Fleet Street and the Strand in medieval times were the great provincial clerics, monastic and military orders, foreigners, and later lawyers and printers. Locations south of the street bordering the Thames were highly prized; the Templars and the Bishops of Salisbury, Durham, Norwich and Lincoln built splendid mansions there with spacious gardens along the river. After the Reformation, favoured members of the nobility, among them the Dukes of Norfolk, Buckingham, Northumberland and the Protector Somerset occupied important sites with their great houses. By the eighteenth century the fashionable centres of residence had moved north and west, and the area of the Strand experienced a relative decline. It was somewhat revived in the 1820s by John Nash's West Strand Improvements, associated with his plan for Trafalgar Square. With the arrival of the railway at Charing Cross Station in 1863 and the subsequent construction of London's largest hotels and of restaurants and theatres, the Victorian Strand became 'the busiest street in Europe'. But the completion of the Victoria Embankment in 1867, isolating the famous southern sites from the river, had a gradual deadening effect, enforced by the construction there in the twentieth century of massive office blocks. The western part of the Strand is now a rather humdrum commercial thoroughfare; properties on the north side have a down-at-heel look, but the growing revival of Covent Garden immediately to the north may once again enliven the street.

To the east are two famous churches, St Mary-le-Strand and St Clement Danes, on unique island sites. Further east, in Fleet Street, lawyers and the press have clung to their traditional positions disposed along the route from the centre of government to the bastion of high finance in the City. The walk ends at Christopher Wren's masterpiece, St Paul's Cathedral.

We begin at the south end of Trafalgar Square, **Charing Cross**, where the statuary and street furniture put up over several centuries indicate what various periods thought to be appropriate markers for this historic site. Charing Cross was a Gothic monument built by Edward I in 1290 to mark the last stopping-place of Queen Eleanor's funeral procession from the north of England to Westminster Abbey. The Cross, torn down by Cromwell's Parliament in 1647, was replaced in 1675 by a statue of Charles I, a work of considerable merit and some delicacy which had lain hidden in St Paul's Churchyard, Covent Garden, during the Interregnum. Around it have gathered a sensitively scaled ensemble of Cast-iron bollards with the insignia of William IV, and later the crest of the City of Westminster, joined by richly Victorian lamp standards.

Northumberland House, built in 1604 and demolished in 1874, stood on the site where the 'nicely besculptured oval stone belly' of **Grand Buildings**

St Mary-le-Strand by James Gibbs and St Clement Danes by Christopher Wren occupy island sites in the Strand. Both steeples are by Gibbs, and both silhouettes are in danger of being further obscured by the City of London's burgeoning mini-Manhattan in the Fetter Lane/Shoe Lane area.
Unprotected view

now curves into the Strand. The main façade of Northumberland House had an extravaganza of Jacobean strapwork as its centrepiece, surmounted by the lion now above the gate to Sion House. The courtyard elevations were coolly Palladian and its interiors were of some grandeur. Grand Buildings has fared better than its predecessor (see Walk 3), but has been stripped of nearly all its Victorian sculptural décor. Westminster's planners have no record of how this happened, but it seems to have occurred some years ago — apparently the determined effort of a former owner to purify his building of 'immoral' eclectic detail. Grand Buildings' façade in Northumberland Street has escaped the modernist's zeal, and should be examined.

The entrance to **Craven Street** south of the Strand is dominated by the hundred-foot-high ventilation shaft of the new Jubilee Line. The shaft's visual impact will be softened by the nine-storey brick-faced office block designed by Hugh Casson for British Rail which will be built north of it. Further south in Craven Street is a row of small, dignified eighteenth-century houses with fine red-brick dressings around the windows.

Adelaide Street north of the Strand presents a view framed by John Nash's St Martin's School, with its graceful Ionic pilasters, and by his 'pepper pots', toward a small group of pleasantly varied buildings in Chandos Place which merit listing as an ensemble. **Charing Cross Station** and Hotel of 1864 have a replica of Edward I's thirteenth-century monument, now a well-established pigeon roost, in the forecourt. The hotel, an ornate variant of the Renaissance palazzo style, was designed by E.M. Barry. Its two top storeys are twentieth-century additions. From the station forecourt there is a striking vista to the dome and cupolas of the National Gallery, and to the steeple of St Martin's, with the double 'pepper pots' in the foreground. The entire Nash block was gutted and a new **Coutts' Bank** is being built behind carefully restored neo-classic façades by Frederick Gibberd. The only regrettable casualty of this otherwise admirable project was MacVicar Anderson's opulent Coutts' Bank of 1903 with its imposing Corinthian colonnades in the centres of Nash's façades. Anderson made a measured drawing out of regard for the Lowther Arcade which his design replaced; Sir Frederick has decorated his garden with remnants of Anderson's listed colonnade.

The Buckingham Arcade penetrates Villiers House, leading down to **Buckingham Street**, site of the Duke of Buckingham's mansion built in 1626 on land formerly occupied by the Bishops of Norwich and then the Archbishop of York. The mansion was demolished when Buckingham engaged the busy developer Dr Nicholas Barbon to put up houses on his property. Canova House, an attractive Italian Gothic design of 1860, with red-brick arches in stock brick walls and big foliage capitals at the entrance, introduces the street. Nos. 17–18 on the east side are Barbon houses with intact façades – elegant red-brick window surrounds, segmental heads, heavy sashes, and Corinthian door cases. Further down on the west side, nos. 13–14 are houses of the 1790s in brown brick; the former has an Adamesque door-case with an ox's skull and shrouds. **York Water Gate** at the bottom of the street was the entrance to the Duke of Buckingham's gardens from the Thames, which extended this far before the construction of the Embankment. The design of 1626, possibly by Nicholas Stone, with heavy-blocked rustication, appears to have been derived from the Italian Mannerist Serlio's design for a gateway published three-quarters of a century earlier, and served as an inspiration for Somerset House's river-front arches.

We return north to John Adam Street; the view east focuses on the white pilasters and pediment of **'The Lancet'**, a remnant of the Adam brothers **Adelphi Terrace**, demolished in 1936 and replaced by an ungainly block in the Manhattan 'Wurlitzer' style. Even though its delicately incised façade was marred by heavy-handed Victorian additions in the 1870s, the destruction of the Adelphi forty years ago still seems a wanton act. The project, begun in 1772 on the former site of the thirteenth-century mansion of the Bishops of Durham, was London's first large-scale speculative housing scheme. It consisted of a long central range framed by side blocks, all of which were raised above the Thames on an arched and vaulted brick sub-structure. Mass-produced patent stone decorative motifs were repeated throughout the terrace. The Grecian palmettes, similar to those found in Portland Place, were stacked vertically in square plaques of cast stone to form the 'honeysuckle' pilasters which remain as the trademark of the Adelphi. The scheme was rashly ambitious, and nearly ruined the Adams financially. The houses were eventually filled by the winners of a government-sponsored lottery, and the vaulted undercroft was let to the Navy as stores.

At the south end of Robert Street, the end pavilion of a side block, no. 3, remains, its stucco crumbling and its pilasters cracking. Another Adam survivor, the **Royal Society of Arts**, 1774, on the north side of John Street has giant order engaged Ionic portico and pediment and a characteristic Adam Venetian window with a radially scalloped stone arch and flattened acanthus leaf capitals, a device which, together with the 'honeysuckle' motif, has been repeated by several Victorian and early twentieth-century buildings further on in the Strand. 'The Lancet', no. 7 Adam Street, further

develops the 'honeysuckle' arabesques on the pilasters in its wrought-iron balcony railings. No. 8, next on the north, has other examples of eclectic detail on the door-case. The Adam brothers drew their decorative motifs from Baalbek and Palmyra in Roman Syria, from Pompeii, Athens and from Diocletian's fourth-century palace at Spalato.

As we return to the **Strand** along Adam Street the vista focuses on a large engaged Corinthian portico, part of Nash's West Strand Improvements. To the east is the Vaudeville Theatre of 1889, a modest, airy design adjoined by small frontages reflecting the Strand's medieval building plots. No. 395 opposite Shell-Mex House is a diminutive mixed Italo-Gothic building of the 1870s. Shell-Mex's red-brick and stone frontage in the Strand is the remaining part of the Hotel Cecil, once Europe's largest, built in 1886 and largely demolished in 1930. It has a big rusticated arch at the entrance and much intricate eclectic detail executed with crisp linearity. The capitals repeat a theme from the Adelphi. In front of Shell-Mex House there are views east to the churches in the Strand and west to the 'pepper pots' and Nelson's Column. To the east are the double turrets of T.E. Collcut's Savoy Court, 1904.

Southampton Street, leading north to Covent Garden, is a typical example of late Victorian street architecture, with textural patterns of brickwork and stone seen in moving perspective together with the gabled skyline, producing the 'optical titillation' so distressing to modernists. The street is made memorable by Edwin Lutyens' large clock projecting from no. 37, and by two houses of 1706, nos. 26 and 27.

Covent Garden was the medieval vegetable garden of the monks at Westminster Abbey. After the Dissolution of the Monasteries, Henry VIII granted the site to the Russell family, later the Dukes of Bedford, in 1552. Francis Russell, fourth Earl of Bedford, commissioned Inigo Jones to design

Inigo Jones' powerful Tuscan portico was originally intended as the entry to St Paul's Church, but in fact never functioned in that way. It now faces hoardings enlivened by school children's murals, pending completion of the GLC's restoration of the Market building and its conversion to a shopping arcade. Parisians lost les Halles; Londoners saved Covent Garden

residences here in 1630. Inigo produced London's first square, a paved piazza in the style of the Italian Renaissance, and not unlike the Place des Vosges in Paris. There were arcaded houses on the north and east sides, the obligatory new parish church, St Paul's, on the west side at the centre, with the gardens of Bedford House on the south. The Earl (later Duke) of Bedford, noted for his vulgarity and miserliness, is reported thus to have described the sort of church he wanted: 'I would not have it much better than a barn.' Inigo gave him 'the handsomest barn in England'. The houses around the square were a commercial success, but the paved piazza was not sufficiently valued for its spatial qualities to ward off the more obvious attractions of trade in lettuce and cauliflower, and in 1670 the Duke of Bedford installed a vegetable market there. One may wonder what the map of central London would now look like if Inigo had planted grass and trees in his piazza instead of paving stones.

The **Market Building** at the centre, now being restored by the GLC as a shopping arcade, was built by Charles Fowler in 1830. The crest above the south entrance bears the Bedford motto 'che sara sara', an appropriate sentiment in view of Covent Garden's changing fortunes. In the eighteenth century the fashionable centre of London moved west, and Inigo's arcaded houses began to be pulled down, replaced by more prosaic structures; the last disappeared in the 1870s. In 1976, the final version of a long series of GLC comprehensive redevelopment schemes, planned to coincide with the removal of the vegetable trade to Nine Elms, was crushed, after ten years of stubborn and determined public opposition. Covent Garden is now recovering from a decade of planners' blight, and if the media consultants, public relations firms, and wine bars now proliferating here are any indication, the area may well become a fashionable centre once again, though that was hardly the intention of the working-class and left-wing groups who led the long struggle against the GLC plans.

In **Henrietta Street** south of St Paul's Church are stucco fronts of the 1850s, covering early eighteenth-century interiors, which form an effective backdrop to the big portico seen from the north. North of St Paul's, Thomas Archer's recently restored no. 43 King Street, 1717, plays the same role seen from the south. The listed eighteenth-century buildings with Victorian fronts in Henrietta Street, nos. 3–10, are being privately refurbished under the watchful eye of the GLC Historic Buildings Division. The Victorian unlisted buildings adjoining on the west unfortunately do not have this protection. They will probably be gutted, though the façades will be more or less retained, an interesting reversal of the Victorians' own procedure.

St Paul's Church was completed in 1633 and restored after fire in 1798 by Thomas Hardwick. Apparently carried away by classical geometry, Inigo planned the church with the entrance through the powerful Tuscan portico on the east, and the altar on the west, reversing the traditional orientation. Outraged church authorities compelled him to turn the plan around during construction. The entrance is on the west side, reached through gates in Henrietta, Bedford and King Streets. The calm interior achieves its effect through the quiet working of its simple proportions.

The late Victorian Bedford Chambers on the north side of the piazza has an arcade recalling Inigo's original houses. At the north-east corner of the square, a wing of E.M. Barry's Floral Hall, 1858, is also arcaded – a Covent Garden theme here executed in cast iron with filigree decoration in the spandrels. The east façade of Fowler's Market Building presents a neo-classic version of the arcade theme – a long balustraded Doric porch four columns deep.

At the south-west corner of Russell Street and Wellington Street, the well-placed polygonal corner tower of the unlisted Edwardian addition to the Flower Market acts as a gatepost along the main axis of the piazza. Its scroll-buttressed Italian Baroque lantern tower and dome are particularly effective viewed from Russell Street to the east, where Samuel Beazley's long porch of

The character of Somerset House's façades vary according to their respective positions. The short Strand frontage is correct and unassertive, the courtyard elevations have an almost domestic quality with elegant porticos and lively rustication. The river frontage, with great arches and Piranesian rustication, is more powerful. (See Walk 5)

fluted Ionic columns, added in 1831 to Benjamin Wyatt's **Theatre Royal**, Drury Lane of 1812, repeats a device familiar from the piazza. Further south in Wellington Street and in Tavistock Street to the east are good eighteenth-century houses. In Wellington and Tavistock Streets on the west is the **Flower Market**, 1887, with an impressive cast-iron glass-roofed hall to be converted for the Theatre Museum. Charles Parnell's **Victoria Sporting Club**, curving into Exeter Street east from Wellington Street, is a lush Victorian stucco palazzo of 1864, now housing the GLC Mechanical and Maintenance Service Division, who ought to devote their professional attention to its façade.

Wellington Street was cut through in 1834 as an extension of the route north from Waterloo Bridge. Where the street curves to join the alignment of the bridge and views open out across the Thames, Samuel Beazley placed the 'Covent Garden porch' of the **Lyceum Theatre**. It projects into the street as a gateway in the manner of John James' portico at St George's, Hanover Square. Historical and spatial continuity were the 'theme and language' of the traditional architects who built Covent Garden.

We return to the Strand, where a red-brick and terracotta mixed north European Renaissance design of 1897 with pinnacles, banded chimneys, and a scrolled gable, rounds the south-east corner leading to the west wing of **Somerset House** in Lancaster Place. James Pennethorne designed this addition to William Chambers' late eighteenth-century block in 1856, faithfully reproducing Chambers' Palladian details and proportions, but adding an ornate frieze, a richly sculptured pediment, and ranks of Victorian statuary to the central portico.

Somerset House, begun in 1776, has its main entrance in the Strand, a quiet Palladian front paying respect to Inigo Jones' river-front gallery which was added to the earlier house built for the Protector Somerset in 1557. Chambers was compelled to demolish the latter when the present building was constructed to house royal societies and government offices. The classical

Remnants of variety and human scale in the Strand stand in the path of an expanding King's College

décor in the three-arched entryway has been augmented by the Adam theme of ox skulls and shrouds, here finely carved rather than cast, and in their normal classical position as metope plaques on the entablature. An eclectic as well as a Palladian, Chambers used Piranesian and Michelangelesque features at Somerset House, particularly in the river front (see Walk 5), but his eclecticism differed fundamentally from that of Robert Adam. Adam varied the elements and proportions of classical orders at will; Chambers kept to the orders and their ratios and found Adam's vagaries a violation of the rules of taste. In the courtyard well-proportioned porticos at the centres of each block show Chambers' mastery of the geometry of classicism, while the triumphal arches with blocked columns leading to side courts indicate his fondness for the devices of Italian Mannerism. The lively pattern of rustication throughout gives an almost domestic warmth to the long façades.

Opposite the main entrance to Somerset House in the Strand are the buildings of the **Aldwych**, an Edwardian redevelopment, completed after the First World War, which connected Kingsway, cut through in 1905, with Waterloo Bridge and the Strand. The buildings are ponderous, their Baroque or classical motifs abbreviated, but the scheme shows a sense of place, particularly at Bush House's curved recession, which respects the island site of James Gibbs' **St Mary-le-Strand**, 1717. The church's interior is a simple hall with an intriguing flat-arched coffered ceiling; the exterior is of considerable delicacy, making the overbearing structural gymnastics and excessive height of the new buildings of **King's College** next to it all the more unfortunate. The college, a branch of the University of London, destroyed precious seventeenth-century timber-framed houses to put up this block in 1966, and hopes eventually to demolish the small eighteenth-

and nineteenth-century houses which lie between its massive block and Somerset House. These frontages are particularly well matched to the scale of St Mary's.

As we proceed east, St Clement Danes and the spires of the Law Courts appear beyond **Australia House**, 1918, a steel-framed block which demonstrates the 'rage for the colossal' which seems to have seized the Baroque Revival just before its extinction. Though overblown, Australia House has been exuberantly sculpted to fit its position. The same cannot be said for its neighbour across the Strand, **Arundel Great Court**, 1976, designed by Frederick Gibberd and developed for the 16th Duke of Norfolk, the Earl Marshal of England, whose family have held the site for centuries. An extensive ensemble of refined red-brick and terracotta buildings designed in the 1890s by John Dunn for the Norfolk Family, and a large and handsome stock brick and stucco palazzo of 1855 in the Strand were all dismissed by Sir Frederick as being 'of no historical interest or architectural distinction', and were razed to make room for the present straight-fronted block of speculative offices with a hotel at the rear. Sir Frederick's design is a curious throwback to the purist temples of American corporate business produced in the 1950s. The undoubted success in their own terms of these works depended upon the care and expense devoted to materials and to the icy perfection of their details. Arundel Great Court seems to have sunk into the lassitude of modernism gone sour. The paving at the entrance to the courtyard would make purists wince, while in the design of the whole space Sir Frederick has succeeded in creating a sense of nameless dread, like the nightmare scenes of early Surrealism.

But there is more, or rather less, to Arundel Great Court than this. According to the architect's own account 'the site is one of the most important in inner London'. The solution intended to provide a 'link' between the churches in the Strand, and was to have the character of an 'Oxford quadrangle' or of the Inns of Court (see the Temple further on, and Lincoln's Inn, Walk 1). The incessant window bands were supposed to 'reflect the general horizontal character of the area', and particularly to refer to Somerset House's 'horizontality'. The building which resulted from this 'townscape analysis' is a kind of ideogram faced in stone, demonstrating the consequences of basing architectural designs upon abstractions breathtaking in their simplemindedness.

Across Arundel Street to the east is Abbey Life House, 1971, also developed for the Dukes of Norfolk. Sir Nikolaus Pevsner describes it as 'a crudely detailed ten-storey block completely disregarding the curve of the street and the scale of its surroundings'. The Victorian buildings which Abbey Life replaced followed the line of the oval circus around **St Clement Danes** laid out by George Dance in 1793. Christopher Wren rebuilt the medieval St Clement Danes in 1682. The steeple above the clock was added by Gibbs in 1719. In 1955 Wren's interior was completely reconstructed by W. Lloyd after war damage. The transition from nave to ambulatory shows Wren's great skill as a pragmatic geometer.

Following Dance's curve south of St Clement's we are presented with a dramatic introductory view of George Edmund Street's **Royal Courts of Justice** in the Strand. The construction of the new Royal Courts of Justice followed a Victorian reorganization of the legal system. A competition was held in 1867 and when Street's winning design was published in 1868, *The Builder* denounced it as 'a deformity and an eyesore for all time', while Professor Fergusson, spiritual father of the techno-fetishists, raged at some length against Street's 'archaeological' design, though when asked to indicate an alternative approach, he could only suggest round instead of pointed arches.

The Courts' main entrance is flanked by twin polygonal towers with faceted slate roofs. On gables above the arches and screen of the entrance are the figures of Solomon holding his Temple on the left, and Alfred the Great,

*Introductory view of the Law Courts
from the west*

founder of English Law, on the right. Above the rose-window of the gabled
Hall at the centre is the figure of Christ. To the east the composition
continues, broken into a series of vignettes, with the gabled blocks separated
by an arched screen. Each block has a set of double pinnacled turrets high
up. A massive clock tower, with the clock projecting on a large moulded
bracket, ends the Strand façade. The composition is carefully adjusted to
angled views along the street, and the impression of the whole is built up
through movement. Two scales operate here: the big rhythms of the various
blocks punctuated by a skyline procession of gables, towers, and turrets, and
the street level rhythm of an arcade, the entrance arches, and a long arched
screen.

The Law Courts seen from Fleet Street to the east

The adjustment of this monumental building to a narrow street further developed the more static picturesqueness found at the Houses of Parliament, and the evolving variety of forms of the Foreign Office at St James's Park. In order to appreciate the importance of Street's design, the Law Courts may be compared with the exactly contemporary Palais de Justice in Brussels, and with the Palazzo della Giustizia of 1888 in Rome. Both are rigidly symmetrical, gargantuan in scale, and overbearing in detail – qualities which set the tone for much subsequent monumental architecture. Street's design, on the other hand, represents a much more advanced, and humane approach, a part of the lost thread of Victorian townscape.

In the Great Hall there is a monument to the architect. Under the Victorian

The Temple Bar's griffin, a mythical beast noted for its voracious appetite, stands at the boundary of the City of London

system of office tutelage he had been the pupil of George Gilbert Scott, and was the teacher of Philip Webb and William Morris. The seated figure of Street bitterly contemplates a sheaf of building plans. Street died in 1881, two years before the building's completion, literally badgered to death by uncomprehending officials.

The Law Courts' long arched screen along the Strand rewards the observant walker with a variety of Gothic foliage capitals, eleven different designs in all. The cement plaster columns, a cheap substitute for Purbeck marble no doubt dictated by cost-conscious officials, must have done their part in driving Street to his grave. The east side and back tower of the Law Courts, faced in red brick with bands and chequers of Portland stone by Philip Webb, may be viewed from Bell Yard and Carey Street to the north. The back tower is well placed facing the gateway to Lincoln's Inn.

The **Temple Bar** opposite the Law Courts' clock tower marks the entrance to Fleet Street, and to the historic core of the metropolis, the City of London. Designed by Horace Jones in 1880, Temple Bar occupies the site of Christopher Wren's three-arched gateway dismantled in 1878.

Fleet Street is a unique phenomenon, a medieval high street, following the curve of the Thames before its embankment, graced by the efforts of intelligent Victorian architects sympathetic to its small frontages, subtle changes of alignment, and changes of level, and not yet ruined by too many modern insertions. The street's extraordinary richness of texture is complemented by changing skyline constellations ruled by the Law Courts' tower and pinnacles, the tower of St Dunstan-in-the-West, and the dome of St Paul's.

No. 1 Fleet Street opposite Temple Bar on the south is a refined Renaissance design of 1879 with discrete rustication. **The Middle Temple Gateway**, 1684, faces Bell Yard leading north to Lincoln's Inn. Its red-brick Palladian design was the work of the lawyer and architectural amateur Roger North. Across Fleet Street at Bell Yard is a branch of the Bank of England, 1888, by Arthur Blomfield, with twin squat corner towers, pilasters and columns of red marble, and heavy grey granite rustication – a building with sombre power beyond its modest size. Next to it at the corner of Chancery Lane is Attenborough's, an Archer and Green design of 1883 richly decorated in red terracotta, the sensuous, 'gustatorial' work of this firm of restaurant architects.

The curved south side of Fleet Street to the corner of Bouverie Street is one of the City of London's small Conservation Areas. The buildings are largely Victorian or early twentieth-century, with much intricate sculptured modelling and variety of material. Notable among them are the **Inner Temple Gate** facing Chancery Lane, a half timber structure of 1611, twice restored; no. 16 just west of it, a tiny slice of a building with an attractive Victorian eclectic stucco front; no. 29, a 'perfectly horrible' design of 1860 with naturalistic ornament; and Hoares Bank, no. 37, a neo-classic block of 1829 in Bath stone.

The Inner Temple Gateway leads to the **Temple Church**. One of the first Gothic structures in England, it was built by the Knights Templar with a round nave modelled on the Holy Sepulchre in Jerusalem. The nave was consecrated in 1185, the chancel added in 1240; both were extensively rebuilt after war damage. The surrounding compounds extending to the Thames were the Templars' headquarters in England. After the Order was dissolved and its leaders burnt for witchcraft in 1312, the Crown granted the area to the Hospitallers, who then leased it to lawyers. For more on the Temple, see Walk 5.

We return to Fleet Street and to the tower of **St Dunstan in the West**. Well placed on the north side at the curve in the street with an open-work lantern and pinnacles, it dominates views from both directions. John Shaw's design of 1829 disregarded traditional orientation, placing the tower and entrance on the south and the brick octagon of the sanctuary and altar on the north.

View west along Fleet Street to the spire of St Dunstan in the West, built at the beginning of the Gothic Revival, and to the Clock Tower and pinnacles of the Law Courts, built towards the Revival's end. Unprotected view

St Dunstan's House was a pleasantly detailed Victorian eclectic design. It has been replaced by the aggressive, over-scaled St Dunstan's Tribunal Courts

Projecting on a bracket next to the entrance is a clock of 1671 from the thirteenth-century church which previously stood here. The figure of Elizabeth I above the vestry porch is from Ludgate, demolished in 1760. The quiet Gothic dignity of St Dunstan's interior, decorated largely with memorial plaques from the medieval church, offers a welcome contrast to the bustle of Fleet Street.

Peele's Hotel, at the corner of Fetter Lane, is a small mid-Victorian palazzo, boarded up and awaiting demolition. There were interesting Victorian structures north in Fetter Lane; nearly all have been pulled down. The most recent to vanish was St Dunstan's House, 1886, demolished by the DOE in 1976.

Fleet Street begins its descent to the valley of the River Fleet, which now runs underground near Ludgate Circus. At Red Lion Court the dome of St Paul's swings dramatically into view. Wren's powerful silhouette dominates the streetscape from here to Ludgate Circus, and the splendid views back to St Dunstan's tower and the Law Courts join in making the procession in either direction among the most memorable in London. Bolt Court leads north to **Gough Square** and to the residence of the eighteenth-century lexicographer Dr Samuel Johnson. The numerous small lanes and courts nearby give a hint of the original medieval scale of the area. We return to Fleet Street along Wine Office Court, past Dr Johnson's famous haunt, 'The Cheshire Cheese', rebuilt in 1667 after the Great Fire.

A group of newspaper buildings, the thumping Egypto-classic Daily Telegraph of 1928, the brash, black curtain-walled Daily Express of 1931 extended east in 1975, and Lutyens' ponderous Reuters/Press Association of 1935 accompany our descent toward Ludgate Circus. A view south to the spire of Wren's **St Bride's**, 'a madrigal in stone', is framed by Lutyens' block and its neighbour to the south. A web of lanes and stairs surrounds St Bride's ancient site, a Roman burial ground built over by Saxon and Norman architects. The early printing trade gathered here, close to the mansions of their steady customers the Bishops of Ely and Salisbury and the Carmelite friars; England's first press with moveable type was located near the old St Bride's. Wren's church was rebuilt after war damage. Seen from the Thames the great height of its spire counterbalanced that of St Mary-le-Bow east of St Paul's.

Ludgate Circus was a coordinated urban design of the 1860s, with buildings on three sides presenting concave faces to the Circus. On the north-east is a stock brick building with foliage capitals, gargoyles, round, segmental and flat lintels, a well-carved, bracketed cornice, and round dormers topped with flowered spikes. Diagonally opposite is a delicate design with pleasantly textured and minutely scaled detail. Ludgate House on the north-west is later and heavier, with a variety of sculptured heads, and a big dome above the corner.

The London, Chatham and Dover Railway flung their bridge across the road, blocking the view to St Paul's. Here we begin our ascent up Ludgate Hill to the cathedral. On the left, at Old Bailey, the rounded High Victorian stucco façade of the former Hope Bros introduces the slightly curved, rising, and angled approach to Wren's west front. The Victorian building is boarded up and awaits the redevelopment of its owners, the Corporation of London. Hope Bros flanks the site of Old Ludgate and marks the position of the medieval city wall. Opposite is a red-brick and terracotta structure by T.E. Collcutt in a style more at home in the West End – Ludgate Hill's only listed building. **St Martin-within-Ludgate** across on the north is a Wren church of 1684 with a slender black steeple serving as a foil to St Paul's west towers and dome. St Martin's interior is centrally planned with the altar skilfully placed on the east. The green seclusion of **Stationer's Court**, with its large plane tree just north of the church rewards the short detour.

The south side of Ludgate Hill was built up in the 1890s. The styles are free Victorian Baroque with much originality and variety of detail. The whole ensemble was carefully considered in its scale, material and curved alignment as part of the sequence leading to the cathedral, and as background architecture it shows an appropriate deference to its mighty neighbour. Juxon House on the north side, a part of Lord Holford's grim **St Paul's Precinct** scheme of 1961, strides into the space in front of St Paul's, and does us the favour of improving the approach to the cathedral by partially blocking it from view.

The cathedral, begun in 1675 and completed thirty-six years later, replaced the old Norman/Gothic St Paul's irreparably damaged in the Fire of 1666. Old St Paul's with a fourteenth-century spire 489 feet high, was the largest church ever built in England. Wren's replacement has been described by some as a flawed masterpiece, by others as a monument to British empiricism. According to Augustus Pugin, 'one half of St Paul's was built to hide the other.' For more on the cathedral, see Walks 5 and 6.

London's most famous vista – from Fleet Street to St Paul's Cathedral

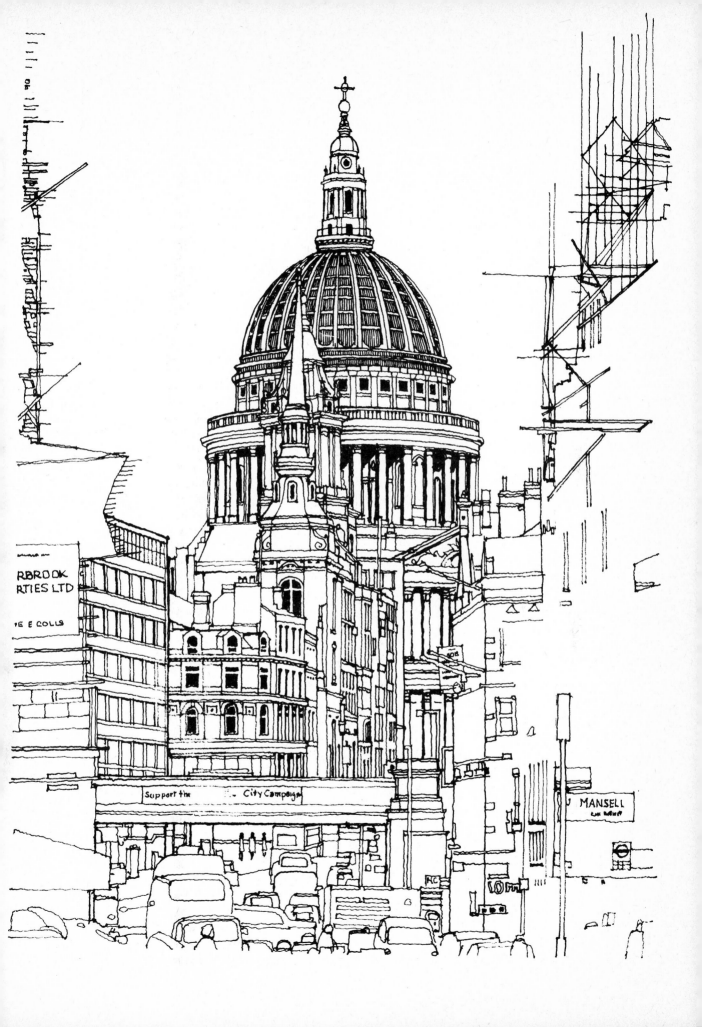

Walk 5 Along the Thames from the Houses of Parliament to St Paul's Cathedral

Old Palace Yard is dominated by the mighty Victoria Tower and its arched royal entrance to the Houses of Parliament. In the middle of the Yard, now the House of Lords' car park, is a Victorian statue of Richard Coeur-de-Lion. The façade of the rest of the Houses of Parliament, elsewhere a regular procession of bay divisions topped by crocketed spires has been here transformed into a complex system of projecting bays, reflecting at larger scale the delicate angled surfaces of Westminster Abbey's Henry VII Chapel opposite.

Across Abingdon Street further south is Henry Yevele's **Jewel Tower** of 1366, the surviving south-west corner of the old Royal Palace at Westminster, with a recreated portion of moat around it. Within the tower are displayed some of the entries in the 1835 competition for the new Houses of Parliament. The Gothic or Elizabethan style was required of all designs; some were heavily symmetrical, others, attempting to be picturesque, were merely confused. Shortly we shall see views from the Thames of the winning design by Barry and Pugin which shows a judicious balance of order and variety.

In the Victoria Tower Gardens is Auguste Rodin's group the *Burghers of Calais*. At Dean Stanley Street west of the Gardens there is a framed view to Thomas Archer's **St John's, Smith Square**, 1728. Thrusting above St John's pediment is the blank concrete end wall of a high-rise slab – the headquarters of the Department of the Environment in Marsham Street. We shall see more of the Department's environmental work from Waterloo Bridge.

Reginald Blomfield was the architectural consultant for **Lambeth Bridge** of 1932. The view south from the bridge is commanded by Ronald Ward and Partners' Millbank Tower, 382 feet high, of 1963. North of Lambeth Bridge is one of London's most stunning riverscapes. Seen from here and from the Albert Embankment further on, the silhouette of Barry's **Houses of Parliament** is at its most handsome. The Victoria Tower, 336 feet high, completed in 1860, is seen in its full height from these angles. Beyond it the

View from Lambeth Bridge to the Houses of Parliament. Barry's silhouette would be marred by high buildings in the vicinity of Leicester Square and Covent Garden. Unprotected view

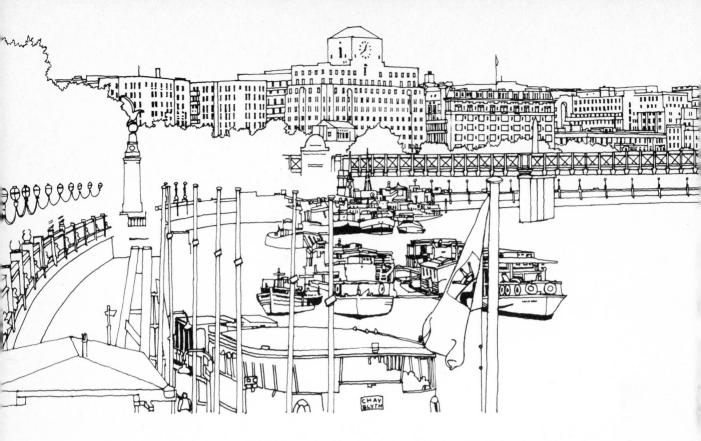

flèche over the central lobby and the clock tower of Big Ben, 320 feet high, completed in 1858, rise above ranks of small crocketed spires and Gothic ventilation shafts. The skyline of the Houses of Parliament has become so familiar as to appear almost inevitable, but Barry's placement of great towers at the back corners of his long river-front elevation was a bold move and virtually unprecedented. The unconventional arrangement avoided the static qualities of a symmetrical composition and produced a silhouette whose most prominent features, changing position in stately procession seen from the river, were precisely sited as the focal points of major street vistas from within the City (see Walks 2 and 3). The design of the Houses of Parliament, like that of the Law Courts in the Strand (Walk 4) was not merely an exercise in Gothic Revivalism; as townscape compositions both were freshly creative works, in their own way, as 'progressive' as the nineteenth-century engineering technologies which have attracted the almost exclusive attention of architectural critics, to the great detriment of twentieth-century townscape.

Beyond the Houses of Parliament are the pinnacles of Archer and Green's Whitehall Court, with a row of stubby blocks following the curve of the Thames in the distance. The Shell Building opposite appears relatively harmless at this range. County Hall, the arcaded pavilions of St Thomas' Hospital, and **Lambeth Palace**, the London residence of the Archbishop of Canterbury, complete the panorama. The palace is largely medieval, with a red-brick gatehouse of 1495, a Hall, also red-brick, rebuilt in 1663 after Puritan demolition, and a neo-Tudor group by Edward Blore completed in 1833.

Before the embankment of the Thames from 1864–70, the river was shallow enough to be forded at Lambeth, and one Member of Parliament is reputed to have walked to work across it. The current was slow and hardly affected by tidal action, particularly before the replacement of old London Bridge, which had acted as a weir. Safe for craft of all sizes, the Thames was a principal traffic artery for passengers and freight. By the mid-nineteenth century, the river had become highly insalubrious; a series of cholera

epidemics claimed thousands of victims, and sewers were finally constructed discharging far downstream. **The Embankment** narrowed the Thames, increasing the swiftness and danger of the current, and taking over much of its traffic, with road haulage replacing barges. The river was left as it still remains, much under-used. Along the Albert Embankment of 1868, and the South Bank further on are lamp standards entwined with fanciful dolphins, repeated from 1870 to 1964.

St Thomas' Hospital's handsome procession of six Victorian blocks, three of which remain, was a design by Henry Currey completed in 1871, with tiers of arcades and corner cupolas, joined at ground level by paired columned balustraded colonnades. The composition is to be replaced by more antiseptic blocks like the one already built at the north end. Opposite is Charles Barry's façade, here seen as an elevation, classically balanced by twin-towered pavilions at either end, with a raised centre position flanked by identical towers. The *flèche* is in the middle; at the far ends are the monumental spires.

Old **Westminster Bridge**, London's second bridge, built in 1749, was a well-proportioned round-arched structure familiar from Canaletto's river scenes. The panorama from the bridge on a radiant morning in 1802 inspired Wordsworth's ode *Upon Westminster Bridge*:

> Earth has not anything to show more fair.
> Dull would he be of soul who could pass by
> A sight so touching in its majesty . . .

A painting by Whistler recorded the demolition of the old bridge, and we step onto its replacement, a graceful cast-iron structure completed in 1862, for views which are more prosaic than those which greeted Wordsworth, but still impressive. To the north-east is the great bend of the Thames. The heavy Victorian cast-iron trusswork of Charing Cross (Hungerford) Bridge is in the foreground; beyond a procession of rather dowdy but not unpleasant Portland stone blocks forming a line of uniform height, with the Shell-Mex clock tower, 1931, as a pivot, follows the sweep of the Victoria Embankment

The great curve of the Thames seen from Westminster Bridge. Unprotected view

and its gardens on the north bank. King's College in the Strand and the new extension to the Law Courts are stacked up behind Somerset House, while the Law Courts spire and clock tower are still just visible above Arundel Great Court. Sticking up further on are some blocks from the City of London's growing high-rise jungle in the Fetter Lane/Shoe Lane district. The South Bank, ruled over by the Shell Building, is more disjointed. **County Hall**, 1911, the headquarters of the Greater London Council, has a static, and despite its mammoth dimensions, rather insipid Edwardian Baroque river front 700 feet long with a concave colonnade at the centre, and Piranesian masonry below. The steep roof and chimneys above create the impression of a much inflated Loire château.

We return to the South Bank promenade, dedicated as a Silver Jubilee Walkway in 1977, past the South Bank Lion, cast in 1837 of Coade stone, the patent artificial stone, its formula now lost, which was used at Bedford Square, Portland Place, and the Adelphi (Walks 1, 2, 4). Seen from in front of County Hall, Norman Shaw's gabled and turreted Scotland Yard blocks opposite, 1890–1906, red brick banded in stone, and the pavilion-roofed Victorian buildings south of them, act in counterpoint to the rhythms and scale of the Houses of Parliament. Views from here past Big Ben into Parliament Square also reveal in sequence the dome of the Methodist Central Hall and Hawksmoor's west towers of Westminster Abbey.

The South Bank Jubilee Garden is a welcome successor to the car park which had occupied the site since the 1951 Festival of Britain. Looming above the garden is the leaden form of the **Shell Building**, 351 feet high, one of the first, and still among the least attractive of the high-rise structures put up following the removal of the 1888 London Building Act's 100-foot height limit in 1956. When the design was exhibited at the Royal Academy that summer it provoked universal condemnation; the London County Council approved it the following year. The result bears an uncomfortable resemblance to Edwin Lutyens' Cenotaph in Whitehall. The Jubilee Bandstand, a lively design in eye-catching orange by Hugh Casson, Conder and Partners, recalls, with its amorphous tentform and 'skylon' supports, the style of the Festival of Britain, which introduced modernism to London here, two decades after its general acceptance on the Continent. Across the Thames is the vigorous silhouette of Whitehall Court and the adjacent National Liberal Club by Waterhouse.

We proceed under Hungerford Bridge and past the gently curved and quietly dignified façade of the **Royal Festival Hall** of 1951 by Leslie Martin and Robert Matthew, substantially altered in the late 1960s, which introduces the South Bank cultural complex. The Festival Hall's tiered foyers and interior promenades have retained their freshness and exhilarating sense of movement. The South Bank complex as a whole has been rightly criticized for isolating the visual and performing arts in 'culture bunkers' cut off from the cafés, restaurants and urban colour in which theatres, galleries and concert halls were traditionally enmeshed. On the other hand the South Bank offers its audiences the decided advantages of a relaxed, traffic-free environment, and of sweeping river views.

The **Queen Elizabeth Hall** complex, designed by the GLC Architects' Department fifteen years after the completion of the urbanely comfortable Royal Festival Hall, is not merely uninviting; its harsh concrete forms bristle with aggression. The design represents the dead end of English Brutalism.

As we approach the concrete terraces of Denys Lasdun's **National Theatre**, 1976, the City skyline with St Paul's dome appears framed by the sweeping arch of Giles Gilbert Scott's **Waterloo Bridge**, 1939, which replaced John Rennie's masterwork of 1817. Sir Denys' theatres, particularly in their suavely handled interiors, remind us, as did the Festival Hall, that the elements of contemporary architecture, if sensitively used, can result in civilized designs. From the National Theatre's terraces there are fine views across to William Chambers' long river-front façade of Somerset House.

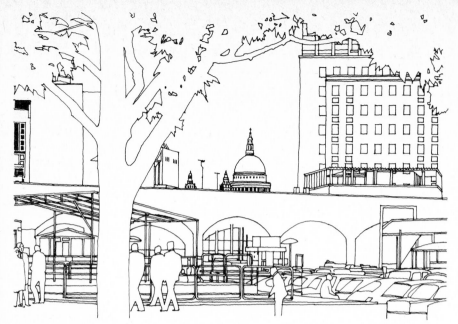

This was the framed view of St Paul's from the South Bank before the insertion of the curiously sited GLC Jubilee Bandstand, which ignores the pedestrian promenade next to it and instead faces the windows of the senior planners in County Hall. In doing so the Bandstand manages partially to block one of the six central London views the GLC was supposed to protect

We ascend the steps to Waterloo Bridge, which spans the Thames at the mid-point of its curve, for dramatic, and in many respects, unhappy views in both directions. To the west, the matchless skyline of the Houses of Parliament has been blurred by the blocks of the DOE in Marsham Street where, it is said, the best laid plans of mice and men are filed away somewhere. The National Theatre to the south-east is dwarfed by high-rise blocks and the effect of its well-considered terraced design is diminished. The South Bank is an area designated as 'inappropriate' for high buildings by the GLC High Building Policy of 1970–76. 'Exceptions', the policy goes on to state, 'will be rare'. Kent House, one of those ubiquitous 'rare exceptions', houses London Weekend Television. It towers over the National Theatre, expressing in a quite unambiguous way the relation between commercial mass entertainment and government-subsidized high culture.

The serenely balanced form of Christopher Wren's dome of **St Paul's**, a parabolic curve which appears hemispheric in perspective, supported on a tall, colonnade-buttressed drum, and surmounted by a high lantern and

The South Bank 'culture bunkers' and Kent House seen from Hungerford Bridge

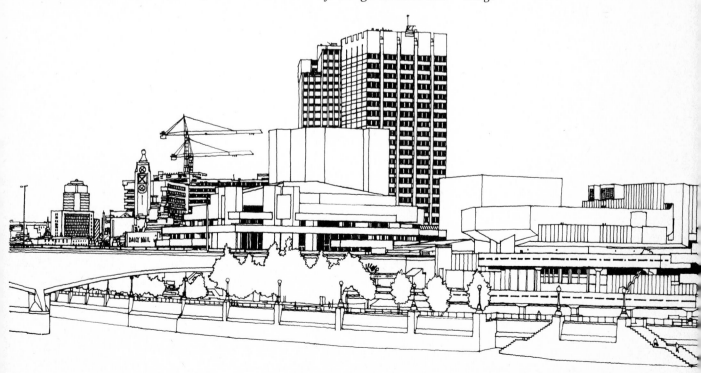

cross, once rose majestically above the spires of his fifty-two City churches, dominating the great visual space of the Thames. Wren's skyline was the architectural expression of the seventeenth-century philosophical and scientific revolution in which England led the world. The law of gravity was first formulated in 1666, the year the Great Fire destroyed old St Paul's. Newton's derivation of the laws of motion led to his invention of the differential calculus, presented in the *Principia mathematica* of 1687, in which he referred to his astronomer colleague Christopher Wren as one of the three greatest geometers of the age.

The cornerstone of Wren's cathedral was laid on 21 June 1675; 36 years later on the same date, the summer solstice, a ceremony at the top marked the

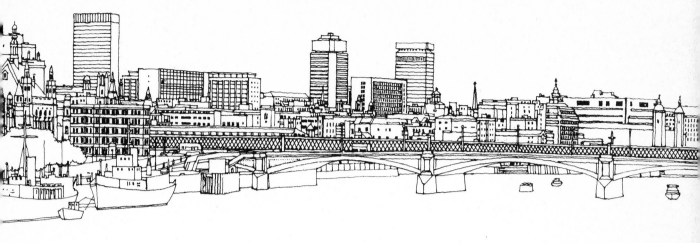

completion of the dome, 365 feet high. The problem uppermost in Wren's mind from the beginning was how to support the weight of the dome and how to counterbalance the tremendous horizontal thrust created by several thousand tons of brick, wood, stone and lead disposed in a double shell around a structural cone. The solution sacrificed qualities of interior space and of 'structural honesty' to an overriding townplanning conception – a planetary system of dome and spires which was unsurpassed in Western architecture.

The Victorian and Edwardian rebuilding of the City raised the Skyline above many of Wren's church spires, but St Paul's dominance remained uncontested until the Faraday Building of 1932 partially blocked its view

View from Waterloo Bridge to St Paul's and the City before the construction of the Nat West Tower. Wren's skyline of dome and church spires expressed the religious convictions of the seventeenth century in terms of Newtonian cosmology. Despite the ravages of high-rise construction since the 1950s, St Paul's retained its dominance on the City skyline until 1977

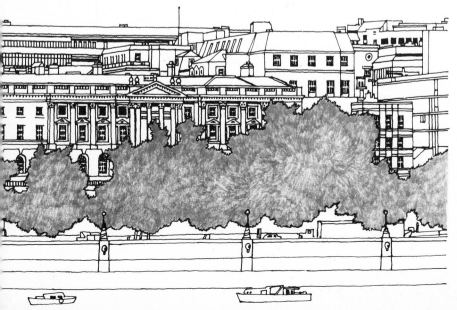

Somerset House seen from the terraces of the National Theatre. Unprotected view

from Waterloo Bridge. In 1935 the City of London issued regulations to protect remaining views from Waterloo Bridge and Bankside further east. The sole purpose of these regulations was to prevent the dome from being blocked from sight; no attempt was made to prevent structures behind or nearby which might obscure or overpower the dome's silhouette. In the 1960s the conglomeration of massive blocks which appeared on the skyline near St Paul's diminished its effect, but none yet dared challenge its dominance.

The final step in the destruction of Wren's skyline was taken by the National Westminster Bank and its architect Richard Seifert. Their 600-foot high black and white striped **Nat West Tower** received the endorsement of the Royal Fine Arts Commission in 1968 and the approval of the GLC in 1970. Recalling Wordsworth at Westminster Bridge, and bearing in mind that poets have long since ceased writing odes to cityscapes, we may be permitted to quote some lines by Shelley to describe the view from Waterloo Bridge to this new giant on the City skyline:

> And Anarchy, the Skeleton,
> Bowed and grinned to every one
> As well as if his education
> Had cost ten millions to the nation.

The Nat West Tower in fact cost one hundred millions, making it the most expensive building per unit area in Europe. *The Times* called the new City skyline the work of 'mad vandals', and the day after Nat West's topping-out ceremony in 1977, a bill was introduced in Parliament calling for more stringent protection of skylines throughout Britain (see page 121).

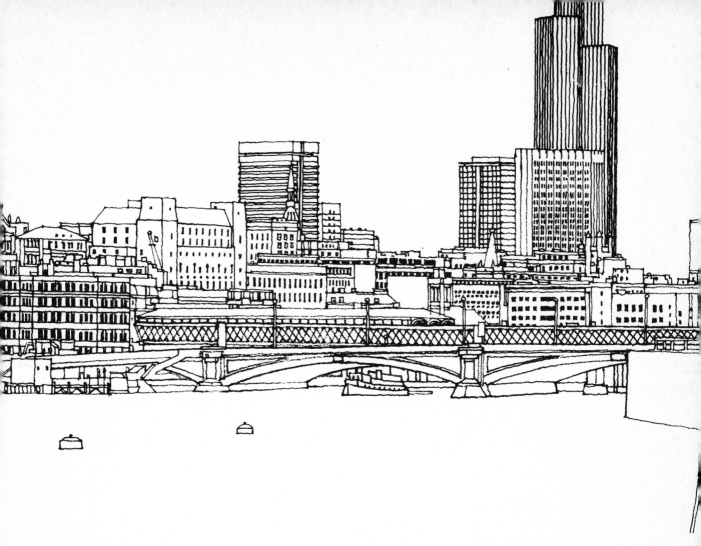

William Chambers' **Somerset House** on the north bank, begun in 1776, has Palladian features repeating those of Inigo Jones' former river-front block and giant Italian Mannerist arches supporting colonnades open to flanking courtyards within. Pennethorne and Smirke added Palladian wings in the nineteenth century. The Strand block of Somerset House once housed the Royal Society, of which Christopher Wren was a founding member. In the Society's former quarters the 1977 'London and the Thames' exhibition displayed artists' changing conceptions of the city and its river. The clarity and coherence of the eighteenth-century views combined breadth of vision with a respect for detail. Vision became blurred and episodic with the rise of Impressionism, grew increasingly subjective and disjointed in the eyes of the Expressionists; and ended in Oskar Kokoschka's energetic, some might say violent panoramas of London's twentieth-century riverscape seen from the top of the Shell Building.

We descend the steps from Waterloo Bridge to the **Victoria Embankment** and proceed east past the heavy rusticated arches at the base of Somerset House's terrace with a monumental water gate at the centre. Like the old Adelphi, Chambers' composition rose directly from the Thames before the construction of the Embankment. Further east, beyond the vacuous modern front of the Howard Hotel, which conceals elaborate repro-Adam interiors of 1976, we pass Herbert Baker's Electra House, its scale reduced by the different character of each tier of windows, and then no. 2, a jewel-like neo-Tudor design of 1895 in Portland stone handled with lush delicacy by J.L. Pearson. To the south on the Embankment is a cast-iron griffin from the City Coal Exchange, demolished in 1963 for road widening which never took place, marking the entrance to the City of London.

The late twentieth-century skyline represents the higher aspiration of homo economicus *and the triumph of his 'dismal science'. The Nat West Tower on the right symbolizes better than any other scheme the heedless extravagance of the 1960s property boom which ended abruptly with the bust of 1973, leaving London with one of the world's most remarkable collections of empty office blocks*

The Temple became Inns of Court when the Knights Templar's headquarters were taken over at the Order's dissolution by the Knights of St John of Jerusalem, the Hospitallers, who leased the complex to lawyers in the fourteenth century. The Temple has retained the character of the medieval episcopal compounds which once lined the Thames; their great houses and spacious gardens opened to the river. The Temple was badly damaged during the Second World War; rebuilding has produced bland copies of the seventeenth-century originals. We enter the complex through the richly carved arched entry of E.M. Barry's Temple Gardens, a corner-turreted French Renaissance design of 1878. Noting the Hospitallers' Lamb and Flag insignia and the Templars' Pegagus on the arch spandrels, we proceed north along the medieval alignment of Middle Temple Lane, above which rises the Law Courts' clock tower in Fleet Street. West of the Middle Temple Hall of 1570 is Fountain Court bounded by intact buildings of the seventeenth century, leading north to Nicholas Barbon's New Court of 1675 framing a contemporary on the north skilfully refronted in the nineteenth century as a stucco palazzo. We return to Middle Temple Lane, proceed south, turn under the arch into Crown Office Row, and move past the green expanse of the Inner Temple Gardens open to the Thames. Ahead is Robert Smirke's austere Paper Buildings of 1838 and beyond in King's Bench Walk are red-brick buildings by Wren and yellow-brick and stone-faced blocks dated 1782 to 1814 flanking the eastern Temple gateway.

East of the Temple is the old **Alsatia** district, site of the vast Carmelite Priory begun in 1241 which stretched from Fleet Street to the Thames. The Carmelite White Friars were a mendicant order and under their protection debtors and an assortment of petty criminals had rights of sanctuary in the priory compound. Officers of the Law who entered to keep the peace were attacked and robbed but the White Friars had no fear of their unsavoury guests, since in medieval times the best burglary insurance was excommunication. The priory was destroyed at the Dissolution in 1545 and rights of sanctuary abolished by Act of Parliament in 1697. A grid of streets lined with solemn and impressive late Victorian structures now occupies the southern portion of Alsatia. The buildings are likely to be blitzed by the new

E. M. Barry's Temple Gardens, which incorporates an ornate gateway to the Inner and Middle Temple, lost its corner turret pinnacle roofs to modernizers. The silhouette of the Temple's roof lines is at the mercy of high buildings in the Fetter Lane area, where the City actively encourages them. Unprotected view

The City of London School and Unilever House seen from the Thames

property speculators' boom now being cooked up, unless the district is granted the status of a Conservation Area which it deserves. Among the buildings notable both individually and in combination are Temple Chambers, French Renaissance with a mansard roof and fine chimneys, 1892; Temple House, stone and red brick, arched windows at ground level, three-storey bays and a corner block tower, 1894; and Telephone House, exuberant Baroque of 1908, all in Temple Avenue. In Tallis Avenue and Carmelite Street are Carmelite House, vigorous streamlined red-brick Jacobethan, 1898, and Horace Jones' Guildhall School of Music with refined eclectic palazzo façades of 1887, extended in 1896, and now boarded up.

We return to the Embankment along John Carpenter Street, past the long side elevation of the **City of London School** which the City Corporation intends to replace with offices and a parking structure. At the Embankment are Arthur Blomfield's red-brick Sion College of 1886, and the big, high-roofed entrance block of the City of London School, by Davis and Emmanuel of 1881, with deeply inset arches on two-storey ranks of engaged columns, a composition well scaled to this important river site. The City plans to retain this façade. We follow the curve of Unilever House's huge soapy block, built in 1931 with slippery-looking rustication and a giant colonnade above reflecting the drum beneath St Paul's dome which here comes into view, framed between the rounded stucco–Gothic corner of Bridge Chambers, 1873, and the remarkable Art Nouveau pub, 'The Black Friar', opposite, with the random green roofscape of *The Times'* former headquarters, Printing House Square of 1963, interceding harshly on the skyline.

Framed vista of St Bride's spire from Carter Lane. Unprotected view

We cross New Bridge Street, enter Queen Victoria Street, and turn north into Blackfriars Lane, leading to the area once occupied by the great medieval Dominican Priory, begun in 1276. The district rising uphill toward the cathedral to the north-east is now largely Victorian, with notable seventeenth- and eighteenth-century enclaves, disposed along lanes, alleys and courts of medieval origin, with **Carter Lane** as a central spine. Lord Holford's plan for the environs of St Paul's treated the Centre Lane ensemble as a *tabula rasa*; a mirror image of the present Precinct was to be installed south-west of the cathedral, and Carter Lane was to become a major traffic artery leading to it. By 1971 the City of London, not noted for excessive solicitude toward traditional architecture, had, under pressure from its Conservation Area Advisory Committee, begun to reconsider Holford's drastic proposals, and even went so far as to create a tiny Conservation Area around Wardrobe Place. On the other hand the cumbersome planning mechanism at County Hall confirmed Newton's First Law: that an inert mass once set in motion will, if undisturbed, continue to bumble on of its own accord. The Greater London Development Plan of 1976, faithfully pursuing the course set by Holford two decades earlier, described the district south-west of the cathedral as 'an environment unworthy of the City's dominant feature, St Paul's', and designated it as an extension of the City's adjacent 'Comprehensive Redevelopment Area', years after nearly everyone else had recognized the area's value and even the City of London had abandoned its schemes for large-scale clearance. The area is now being rehabilitated and it seems unlikely that the GLC's vision of windswept piazzas here will be realized.

Playhouse Yard commemorates the theatre built after the Dissolution over the ruins of the Dominican Priory, and used by Shakespeare's company before local residents drove them across the Thames. On the east side of Blackfriars Lane near the junction with Apothecary Street is a Tuscan doorcase and broken pediment framing the barrel-vaulted entry to the **Apothecaries' Hall**, built in 1671 on the foundations of the Blackfriars' medieval guesthouse. The courtyard elevations were stuccoed and a pediment added facing the entry in 1786.

We proceed up Ludgate Broadway past an area vacant since the Blitz, and turn east into Carter Lane. Nos. 79–81 on the south are small houses built after the Fire and stuccoed in the nineteenth century; then comes Church Entry leading to the site of the Blackfriars' preaching nave; and then the descending meander of St Andrew's Hill, leading to Wren's **St Andrew's by the Wardrobe**. Further east in Carter Lane is **Wardrobe Place**, a cobbled rectangular court of great charm. Its eighteenth- and nineteenth-century buildings display a variety of brick colours. The badly maintained Rennaissance façade of St Paul's Choir School, 1875, leads to Dean's Court and Wren's red-brick Deanery of 1670 with moulded brick dressings, timber eaves, and a steep roof. The Baroque corner turret and copper dome of the 1890s ahead marks the entrance to St Paul's Churchyard and the cathedral's west towers and portico here come into view.

Walk 6 begins at St Paul's west front.

Apothecaries' Hall. The well-proportioned enclosure and the graphic pattern of round windows, clockface, crests, and a large and handsome wrought-iron lamp standard make the courtyard one of London's hidden treasures

Walk 6   The City of London

Over the course of centuries, while the centres of political and religious administration, of learning, entertainment, and residence moved elsewhere, the craftsmen, merchants and financiers of the City of London have remained steadfast in their commercial pursuits, jealously guarding the political and fiscal autonomy first demanded of William the Conqueror by the Saxon burgesses and expanded by the twelfth- and thirteenth-century Royal Charters granted to London's trader-citizens.

The City's market places now deal in information rather than goods: the livery companies, still the basis of the City's electorate, have retained a nominal connection with the medieval guilds of craftsmen and merchants whose colourful crests they bear, but are now societies composed largely of bankers and brokers. The City's commercial pre-eminence, once based on access to land and water transport, now derives from the proximity of a great variety of information markets and financial services, tied together in the 'delicate web of understandings' which make the Square Mile a world centre of foreign exchange and commodity transactions, of banking, ship brokerage and insurance. Today more than ever, the business of the City is business.

The City began as a Roman legionary camp set up shortly after the invasion of Britain in 43 AD. The legions' surveyors who laid out the settlement on a secure gravel plateau above the Thames' marshy floodplain chose their site well. The river here was no longer affected by tides and was easily bridged to the well-drained heathland to the south. The intersection near the present London Bridge of an important regional land route with water-borne transport coming up the Thames estuary from the Continent made Londinium a hub of strategic communications soon celebrated for its traders. After the cult of emperor worship centred here, the city became the capital of Roman Britain. The wall surrounding Londinium was rebuilt in Saxon and medieval times; traces of it are still visible. Newgate and Aldgate at either end of the City's main east–west thoroughfare are known to have Roman origins. The legionary grid of streets with a forum and basilica near the present Leadenhall Market disappeared with the decay of Londinium accompanying the collapse of the Roman Empire and with the havoc wrought by Danish invaders in the ninth century. The grid was replaced by a Saxon and Norman system of sinuous main thoroughfares crossed by tiers of small lanes descending to the river, and interconnected by even smaller alleys. These together form the basis of the City's present street pattern.

Medieval London had already spread well beyond the wall before the Plague of 1665 and the Great Fire of 1666 accelerated the flight to the suburbs. A grand Baroque layout proposed by Wren to replace the five-sixths of the City devastated by fire was rejected. Brick houses, constructed according to new fire codes prohibiting traditional half-timber, were quickly put up along the old street lines. Despite the rejection of his rationalist town plan, Wren's contribution of St Paul's and fifty-two City churches, twenty-three of which remain, is an unparalleled achievement.

A wave of Victorian and Edwardian redevelopment replaced most of the City built after the Fire and converted nearly all of its remaining residential quarters to commercial use. The nineteenth-century City was built to such density that daylight became as precious as water in the desert. It was hoarded and collected in countless skylights, light wells, and reflectors. The Victorian architects working in the City set examples for the rest of London

in the quality, ingenuity, and variety of their designs, and important variants of Victorian architecture developed with the rise of imperial commerce. A lush proliferation of styles – rich Victorian classicism with its allusions to the Baroque of Venice, Second Empire eclectic palazzi with their growing emphasis on skyline, sombre polychromatic gothicity and Italian medievalism, conjuring up images of princely merchants as well as responding to Ruskin's exhortations, and the charming vagaries of Norman Shaw's red-brick 'Queen Anne Revival' – began here.

The Victorians wove a harmonious urban fabric out of buildings which, considered individually, displayed extraordinary variety and individuality. Edwardian works and those of the 1920s enlarged the scale and reduced the fantasy, but continued to respect the medieval street alignment so that even their larger façades seen in changing angles of perspective still deflected the eye along the continuously evolving vistas which for a thousand years had been an essential feature of the City's unique townscape. That quality is now largely lost; present views focus with stupefying effect upon the fixed hulks of high-rise blocks.

A third of the City was destroyed during the Second World War. Although postwar replacements were disappointing, it was not until the property boom of the 1960s and 70s that a large part of London's historic core became what many consider to be an architectural disaster area. The basic ground rules of alignment, scale and skyline were utterly disregarded. A former City fireman, Mr John Horner, described his reaction to a report on the City's latest surge of redevelopment in this letter to *The Times*: 'The climax of the Nazi fire raids on the City came on December 29, 1940. Churchill sent a message to the firemen – "Save St. Paul's". The New Year dawned with most of the area north of the Cathedral as far as Moorgate a smoking ruin; eight Wren churches gone; two City Livery Halls gutted; Paternoster Row, with its millions of books, in ashes. The Cathedral Chapter House was burnt but the Cathedral stood scarred but safe. Now you tell us that, six hundred feet high, a Seifert slab will overtop the Cross. The war memorial of the Fire Brigades Union carries lines from William Morris:

> There in the world new builded
> Shall our earthly deeds abide
> Though our names be all forgotten
> And the tale of how we died.

The City skyline from St Bride's, circa 1974. Bits and pieces of the City's unique ambience remain, enough to intrigue the visitor and to merit the redoubled efforts of conservationists. Some townscape ensembles and several fine buildings have survived both blitz and boom. Unfortunately these must now be appreciated as isolated works and not as they were intended, as parts of a coherent and civilized urban fabric

The western approach to St Paul's up Ludgate Hill. The former Hope Bros. block, foreground left, has been vacant and decaying for five years. The property is owned by the City, who prefer to redevelop rather than rehabilitate the building. Since the site lies within a Conservation Area, the City's own plans are indicative of its understanding of conservation

"Newbuilded"? Those of us with the fire service in the City on those winter nights of 1940/41 thought it would be so. Reading *The Times* (1 March 1975) I felt we might as well have let it all burn. It would have saved the grabbers and the developers a lot of trouble and money and made it much easier for their "architects". Certainly many a good fireman we lost in the City those nights might now be drawing his well-earned fire brigade pension.'

As we begin our townscape walk at the west front of St Paul's, it should be noted that what remains of the City's architectural heritage is still seriously under-protected. Listed buildings are sparser in the City than in most other parts of central London, a good many valuable Victorian and Edwardian works have not been registered, and the expanded City list drawn up in 1974 disappeared for four years down the nameless corridors of the Department of the Environment. Once listed, buildings are still hardly safe: 'listed building consent', ie permission to demolish, is more easily obtained in the City than anywhere else in London. Listed interiors are gutted as a matter of course, and total demolition occurs often enough to cause serious concern. The City's Conservation Areas are miniscule, and even they, as we shall see, are being subjected to large-scale clearance.

Old **St Pauls** was a gigantic Romanesque and Gothic structure built on the site of a church founded by Bishop Mellitus in 604 and destroyed by fire in 1087. Inigo Jones encased the Romanesque nave in Palladian stone-work and added a monumental classical portico on the west in 1630, but when a Royal Commission which included Christopher Wren examined the cathedral in 1666 a few days before the fire, they found it in a ruinous state. Though the fire damaged the old structure beyond repair, gunpowder and battering rams were required to demolish its massive ruins.

The 1673 Great Model design for the new cathedral preferred by Wren and Charles II was a structure centrally planned according to the Renaissance ideal, with a great hemispheric dome above the crossing. It was rejected by the clergy on liturgical grounds, and in order to get the project under way, Wren then submitted a prosaic Latin-cross plan with a curious shallow dome, squat lantern and staged octagonal spire. The external walls were stepped, reflecting the difference in height between side aisles and nave, and resembled Inigo's demolished Palladian elevations. The design was approved by Royal Warrant in May 1675 with the stipulation that the architect would be allowed to make changes 'ornamental rather than essential' as he saw fit. Wren clearly had no intention of adhering to the Warrant Design as the masons must have realized when they laid foundations in June 1675 for walls two feet thicker than those of the Warrant. The extra thickness was required to support external walls which rose as screens to the height of the nave concealing the differences in roof level within, and hiding the flying buttresses, 'shameful little things', which braced the vaulting of the nave. Wren also conceived the heavy external walls as buttresses remitting the enormous thrusts of a dome even higher and grander than that of the Great Model. A consequence of the thickened outer walls was the unequal spacing of the interior piers supporting the dome at the crossing. It will become apparent when viewing the cathedral's interior that Wren's solution to the awkward visual and structural problems arising from this arrangement cost him much effort.

The angled approach to the cathedral up Ludgate Hill frames its south-west tower and clock face, and then the unusual two-level portico with paired columns supporting a pediment which bears a relief sculpture of the conversion of St Paul. His figure stands above at the apex. The disposition of the cathedral's forms and of a system of ornament subtly scaled in response to street-level views was based on Wren's firm conviction that 'the Architect ought, above all things, to be well skilled in Perspective; for every Thing that appears well in Orthography may not be good in the Model; and everything good in the Model may not be so when built; but this will hold universally true, that whatsoever is good in Perspective will be as good in great, if only this Caution be observed, that Regard be had to the Distance of the Eye.'

The cathedral's dominant townscape features are the west towers and the dome, all designed in their final form about 1704. The dome on its high colonnaded drum is a work of great visual repose, the towers are masterpieces of Baroque design related to Borromini's Sta. Agnese in Rome. Square towers above the main cornice support drums ringed by colonnades with paired columns projecting diagonally. Their entablatures bear bands of huge egg and dart, sized for 'the Distance to the Eye'. Ogee cupolas above openwork scroll buttresses culminate in great gilded acorns.

Wren's use of ornament at St Paul's deserves special note for the way in which it fulfils his dictate about perspective and humanizes the cathedral's great stone mass. Small panels below the round-arched windows of nave, transepts and choir display particularly delicate carving near eye level; the keystones of the windows above are graced by a variety of cherubs' heads. Beneath the lower entablature running round the building are festoons of fruit and floral garlands at the level of the capitals, recalling similar decoration at Inigo Jones' Banqueting House (Walk 3). The lower entablature is plain with a band of fine egg and dart. At the upper level frieze there are strongly grooved scroll brackets supporting a cornice and balustrade. The interior system is similar, but the lower entablature is completely plain, while the cornice below the vaulting is lushly elaborate. The paired pilasters and columns of the exterior are Corinthian below and Composite above; the arrangement is reversed inside.

The interior, despite its vast dimension, creates an impression of light and elegance. Much of the carving inside and out is by Gibbons, Cibber and Kempster. Just inside the entrance next to the south-west tower the Chapel of St Michael and St George recalls the traditional dedication of west towers to the saints who were to defend the Holy City against the western approach of the forces of evil, according to the prophecy of Daniel. From beneath the dome the view upwards reveals part of Wren's three-layer construction. The inner dome is a plastered brick shell; above it the outer lead sheathing is borne on timber trusswork, and between the two a structural cone of brick does the main work of supporting the high stone lantern. The ascent within the dome to the lantern is for climbing enthusiasts; it reveals the intricacies of Wren's construction and presents sweeping views of London.

In 1718, at the age of eighty-six, Wren was accused of mismanagement and dismissed as Surveyor-General, a post he had held for forty-nine years. The Latin inscription under the centre of the dome informs us that he produced the greatest architectural work in London '... not for himself, but for the public good. Reader, if you require a monument, look around you.'

North of St Paul's west front the Paternoster Steps lead up to Lord Holford's **Precinct**, built between 1961–7 on the site of Paternoster Row destroyed in 1940. The centrepiece of Paternoster Square is an eighteen-storey slab block deliberately placed here as a demonstration that high-rise blocks near the cathedral would not diminish the dome. The building was tragically mis-sited; it cruelly blocks Wren's skyline from the Farringdon Street approach and appears flung across the dome seen from London's most famous vantage-point on Parliament Hill in Hampstead. Leaving the Precinct, we move east along St Paul's Churchyard. On the north is Wren's red-brick chapter house of 1670, now restored. Cast-iron railings of 1714 enclose the semi-circular portico of the north transept, and the old churchyard. Opposite St Paul's on the east is the diminutive lead-hatted choir school, and further east across New Change is the gently curved red-brick neo-Georgian façade of the Bank of England extension, 1960, roundly condemned as 'retardataire', but surely better suited in material and layout to the environs of St Paul's than Holford's bleak Precinct.

We leave the churchyard by the north-east gate and proceed across Cheapside towards the tower of St Vedast, Foster Lane, well framed by two otherwise undistinguished postwar blocks. **Cheapside** to the east is part of the City's main east–west thoroughfare and has been the City's main shopping street since medieval times. The names of adjacent streets – Bread Street, Milk Street and Poultry – attest to the markets which clustered here. The view east is punctuated by the spire of Wren's St Mary-le-Bow and terminates in the corner dome of MacVicar Anderson's Royal Insurance Group at the Bank intersection. To the north-west is the handsome steeple of **Christ Church, Newgate Street**, 1691, a square, open colonnaded lantern and pinnacles rising above segmental pediments, topped by a slim square spire and cupola. The tower is the remnant of one of Wren's most splendid churches. The nave was burnt out in 1940 but the external walls remained intact and restorable until the City of London and Post Office planners took up where the Luftwaffe left off and converted the shell to what they call 'a noble ruin' by shoving a realigned King Edward VII Street through the body of the church to accommodate the bureaucratic bulge of the new Post Office Headquarters which will also block London's best street vista of St Paul's dome from the north.

Wren's **St Vedast**, 1700, was also gutted during the war, but its interior, a simple hall with a flat ceiling on coved edges, and a serenely proportioned chapel on the south behind a Roman Doric arcade, has been beautifully restored. History, looking back, may well consider the many lovingly rebuilt Wren churches as the most valuable architectural contribution of the postwar City. St Vedast's steeple is Wren's most Baroque, with the concave profile below becoming convex above. Its sculptural strength was once seen together with several other quite different spires nearby. Medieval London was remarkable for its numerous small parish churches, ninety-seven within the walls before the fire, and Baroque London was fortunate to have so many of them replaced by an architect with a taste for variety and an experimental turn of mind.

Opposite: these before and after views of St Paul's from King Edward VII Street demonstrate the effect of the (Royal Fine Arts Commission approved) design for the new Post Office headquarters upon fine vistas of the Cathedral. Unprotected view

Foster Lane leads north past modest Georgian and Victorian structures on the east side to a bend where Philip Hardwick's **Goldsmiths' Hall** of 1835 comes into view. Hardwick's pilasters and demi-columns bear what must be the most magnificent Corinthian capitals in London, with luxuriantly spreading acanthus leaves. Beneath the entablature of the engaged entrance portico are equally sensuous large-scale heraldic crests, making the design, with its references to the Baroque of Venice, an introduction to the prosperous exuberance of the Victorian era.

Opposite on the north-west is **St Anne and St Agnes**, a simple red-brick Wren church of 1680, restored after bombing. The south side of this centrally planned structure has a pediment raised high above a large central round-arched window trimmed with orange dressed quoins. The small square tower at the west end, surmounted by a tiny timber lantern and leaded cupola, is visible from the intimate and well-landscaped churchyard on the south.

We turn east in Gresham Street and proceed toward Wren's **St Lawrence Jewry** which dominates the vista. As we approach the steeple, a sombre leaded bell turret at a different angle from the pinnacled stone tower below it, the ubiquitous Nat West Tower swings into view behind, and the new Guildhall extension over-exerts itself immediately north of the church. St Lawrence, completed by Wren in 1687 and restored after war damage, is the Guild Church of the Corporation of London. The corporation's governing body, the Common Council, is elected according to the medieval system by the liveries of the guilds who comprise about 8000 of the City's 400,000 commuter-workers. Entering the Guildhall's new piazza past the north-east corner of St Lawrence, we are confronted with the monolithic Alderman's Court, a highly improbable stone-faced form on stubby legs sticking out from the main block of the Guildhall extension, a gymnastic contraption of 1974 by the firm of Giles Gilbert Scott. The quietly dignified **Guildhall** to the north-east was begun in 1411, the 'Gothick' entrance façade of 1789 is by Dance the Younger, the roof and *flèche* of 1861, restored by Giles Gilbert Scott after bomb damage, are by Horace Jones. The central spires above Dance's fanciful Greco-Gothick entrance flank a pair of griffins clutching a crest bearing the City emblem, the Cross of St George. 'Domine dirige nos', the City motto, is inscribed below. A scheme by the City Corporation to demolish Dance's front was blocked in 1964, but Dance's Justice Room, which together with the City Art Gallery enclosed an entrance court 'gratifyingly informal and intimate in the best tradition of the City' (Pevsner), was pulled down in 1969 to create the present open space.

We proceed south from the Guildhall past the diminutive neo-classic Irish Chamber of 1825, stucco blind arcades below, brickwork above, on the east. St Lawrence Jewry's engaged Corinthian portico on the west, with arcaded niches and round-headed windows beneath festoons at column capital level, recalls St Paul's ornamental system. **King Street** and Queen Street further south were laid out by Wren on the axis of the Guildhall entrance. A chamfer-cornered free Victorian palazzo of 1852 by Sancton Wood south-east of St Lawrence accompanies our walk south along King Street with well-textured rustication and segmental arches on Tuscan columns at ground level. Next to it, a few years later in time and some centuries earlier in style is the stock brick Italian medieval Banco do Brasil. As we approach Cheapside a glance back to the Guildhall shows a curtain-wall block of the London Wall development rising above the *flèche*. **Atlas House** at the intersection with Cheapside on the north-east is a carefully considered astylar palazzo by Thomas Hopper of 1836 with rusticated arches, cornices at lower and upper levels, and pleasingly miniaturized detail. The arcade framing the Cheapside pavement was part of postwar restoration work. Cheapside to the west is dominated by Wren's highest and most famous City church steeple, the spire of **St Mary-le-Bow** of 1683. The tower, projecting north of the body of the church, which maintains traditional orientation, has at its base large arched

A close-up of the Mappin and Webb corner

niches with distinctive scalloped voussoirs framing Roman Doric door-cases. Voluted pinnacles above the corners of a square tower help make the visual transition to a round lantern which rises like a small colonnaded temple. Its balustrade is surmounted by twelve inverted scroll brackets which from a distance appear as a ribbed dome and from close range repeat in classical form the 'bow' arches on the pre-Fire tower which gave the church its name. The brackets taper gracefully to a slim stepped square tower topped by a pyramid spire, ball and flying dragon weathervane.

On the south side of Cheapside to the east, which here becomes Poultry, the diagonal intersection of Bucklersbury marks the beginning of a noteworthy block of small commercial structures which retain the character of the Victorian and Edwardian City. The corner block of 1875 at Bucklersbury is in the red-brick 'Queen Anne' style introduced two years before by Norman Shaw at New Zealand Chambers in Leadenhall Street; Shaw's red-brick architecture had a considerable influence upon the character of the West End, but examples of the style are rare in the City. The architects of this block were J. & J. Belcher who also designed the important corner building of **Mappin and Webb** at the east end of the ensemble. Between the end blocks a fine procession of façades display individuality, fantasy and good manners. The styles include late Georgian, Romanesque, Italian Gothic and Edwardian Baroque. The ensemble's materials are a colourful mixture of red brick, terracotta, Portland and Bath stone, and stock brick. The townscape importance of the group merits the protection of a Conservation Area which the City's planning committee still declines to grant it, despite the fact that a developer's scheme for total clearance and replacement by a twenty-storey office block seems to have been indefinitely postponed.

At the Bank intersection to the east, the rounded corner of MacVicar Anderson's fine Edwardian townscape design, with emphasized banded rustication below and a ribbed dome above, holds our view as we proceed towards it. On the north side of Poultry Edwin Lutyens' **Midland Bank** of 1924–39 is a strongly sculptural work with an arcaded base and tiers of windows above set in three-storey arches. The continuous horizontal bands of rustication which step subtly back as they rise add to the perspective effect of this masterly piece of street architecture, equally impressive when seen in angled views from Lombard Street to the east.

Queen Victoria Street was cut through in 1871, creating the triangular site occupied by J. & J. Belcher's Gothic block of 1870, with its turreted corner

A view of the Bank junction from the Royal Exchange. On the left is the Mansion House and right of it is the Mappin and Webb block, clothed in scaffolding for 'temporary renovation'. Mappin and Webb and its neighbours in Poultry were to be demolished to make room for a Mies van der Rohe office block facing a Leicester-Square-sized piazza (see p. 105). The plan seems to have been finally dropped

facing MacVicar Anderson's dome on a similarly shaped site opposite. Ahead is the Lord Mayor's residence, **Mansion House**, a Palladian design by Dance the Elder of 1752 with a raised Corinthian portico facing the Bank intersection to the north. Before inspecting the commercial hub of the City, we turn south at Mansion House into Walbrook, named for the stream once at the centre of Roman London, towards Wren's **St Stephen Walbrook**, begun in 1672. The interior is his most spatially complex and adventuresome; the dome on eight pendentives was designed at the time of the Great Model scheme for St Paul's. The delicate spire of 1717 was one of Wren's last.

We return north along Walbrook, towards Edwin Cooper's **National Westminster Bank** of 1932. The 'neo-classic' designs of the 1920s and 30s elsewhere in London tended to abbreviate and then eliminate traditional motifs, but the Bankers' classic designs in the City such as this one maintained an image of dignified rectitude with authentic detail. Cooper's block repeats Lutyens' continuous horizontal rustication and banded stonework.

The irregular space formed by the convergence of seven main thoroughfares south of the Bank of England is the heart of the City. Unlike Piccadilly Circus and Trafalgar Square, the Bank junction was never laid out

View looking west along Poultry to MacVicar Anderson's domed corner block. On the left is Lutyens' Midland Bank, on the right is the Mansion House. A 1960s Brutalist tower looms in the distance

The effect of the Commercial Union Building, winner of a Civic Trust design award, upon the silhouette of the Royal Exchange (below)

as an urban space; it simply evolved as the Royal Exchange, the Bank of England and Mansion House were successively sited here. Like the Circus and the Square, the junction lacks a homogeneous sense of spatial enclosure; movement dominates, and the character of vistas varies greatly with change of position.

Between 1788 and 1808 John Soane built an extended **Bank of England** on the site of an earlier bank building completed in 1734. His highly inventive domed banking halls encased in a windowless perimeter wall fell victim to further expansion of the Bank when Herbert Baker replaced Soane's halls with the present graceless ten-storey mass rising above the retained exterior screen. The wall is balustraded, with curved corners and Corinthian colonnades in porticos or ranked in front of recesses. The stonework shows no vertical joints, creating the impression of unbroken horizontal bands.

The present **Royal Exchange** of 1843 by William Tite is the third to occupy the site. The first was founded by Thomas Gresham in 1566 as a centre for commercial transactions similar to the Bourse in Antwerp. Tite's commanding eight-columned Roman temple front was clearly intended as the centrepiece of the Bank intersection, and countless Victorian prints show how well it fulfilled this function. Seen from the principle vantage-point at Mansion House, the dominant role has been taken over by the **Stock**

Opposite: Looking west from Cornhill towards St Paul's, partially obscured by a ten-storey block in Cheapside

The same view as it would appear if Mies' Chicago block, mentioned on p. 102, had been built. The scheme had the approval of the City Corporation and the Royal Fine Arts Commission

Exchange, thirty-four storeys of drab concrete, and by Richard Seifert's gigantic zebra-striped Nat West Tower.

We proceed from Mansion House east into Lombard Street, passing the rusticated bands of Anderson's Royal Insurance Group of 1905. Its listed interiors are being gutted for redevelopment. At the apex of Lombard Street and King William Street stands the ruggedly individualistic Guild Church of **St Mary Woolnoth**. T.S. Eliot referred to the church in *The Waste Land*:

> And each man fixed his eyes before his feet.
> Flowed up the hill and down King William Street,
> To where Saint Mary Woolnoth kept the hours. . . .

We raise our eyes to the most original of the City churches, designed by Wren's most brilliant pupil Nicholas Hawksmoor and completed in 1727. Twin square balustraded towers rise above the entablature of a high-level colonnade. At the base a round-arched entrance and semi-circular window are scalloped into the unbroken bands of rustication which continue around great Tuscan columns flanking the west front. Hawksmoor's strongly incised bands are the source of the theme repeated over the following two centuries by the architects of major buildings around the Bank junction.

St Mary's clock projects over **Lombard Street**, named for the money-changers of Lombardy who took over the City's foreign exchange dealings after the Jews were expelled in 1291. The street is hung with the shields and insignia of today's bankers. The converging curves of **St Edmund the King's** leaded spire rise to the east; beyond is the awkward curtain-walled Kleinwort Benson block in Fenchurch Street. Pope's Head Alley leads us from the north side of Lombard Street into Cornhill. We emerge next to the Royal Exchange's entrance portico, and facing the central colonnade of the Bank of England. The courtyard of William Tite's Exchange, glass-roofed in 1880, presents the full richness of Victorian eclectic classicism. The view from the steps of the Exchange confirms the vital townscape role of the unlisted Mappin and Webb corner block in Poultry.

Cornhill to the east frames views back to St Paul's dome. Opposite the piazza at Royal Exchange Buildings is the recently refurbished Banco Nazionale di Lavoro in Cornhill, a palazzo of 1857 by the Francis Brothers, architects of Grand and Trafalgar Buildings in Trafalgar Square (see Walk 3). The façade is framed by the piazza and consists of block-rusticated Roman Doric demi-columns at ground level, tiers of pedimented, flat-entablatured and round-arched windows, the latter with floral spandrels above and panels of garlands and arabesques below. Then comes a luxurious cornice on double scrolled brackets with rosettes between on the frieze, a leaded mansard with dormers and a skyline of wrought-iron floral spikes. The inspiration for the design was the Italian Renaissance by way of the Parisian Second Empire – a work of resourceful eclecticism rather than academic reproduction.

The view north from the piazza presents an assemblage of heavies on the skyline: the leaden-grey Stock Exchange, the polished granite 'slickist' Angel Court tower, and Richard Seifert's curved Drapers' Gardens block, with bands of iridescent green windows.

Turning east into Threadneedle Street, and then north at Bartholomew Lane, we reach **Throgmorton Street**, one of the most remarkable small Victorian ensembles in the City. The new Angel Court complex introducing the street on the north side replaced a substantial Victorian enclave designated a Conservation Area after it had been demolished. The remaining procession of intricately detailed façades on the north side in varied materials and styles take full advantage of the street's curve to produce a memorably textured sequence. **Drapers' Hall**, red-brick neo-Jacobean of 1898 with a variegated skyline, is the dominant building; nos. 27 and 27a are individualist's classic and Baroque; no. 26 is carefully incised orientalized Italianate; and no. 25 is a fascinating Venetian Gothic design of 1869. Above all this pleasing confusion the black and white stripes of Europe's tallest office building thrust into the stratosphere.

Philip Hardwick's Italianate stucco **City Club** of 1834 in Old Broad Street to the north was to be demolished to clear the way for yet another Nat West Tower, but was reprieved by a last minute 'spot-listing' in 1974. It now seems likely that Hardwick's threatened interiors, which the Victorian Society considers 'noteworthy for a combination of splendid proportion and dignified restraint', will be retained. An archway opposite Throgmorton Street leads from Old Broad Street to Adam Court, a small medieval alignment leading east and then north to the balustraded triangular courtyard and fountain, facing the City Club's elegant east façade with its three large and handsome Venetian windows.

We emerge from Adam Court into Threadneedle Street near the intersection with **Bishopsgate** to the east, the medieval City's principal route from London Bridge to the north. Bishopsgate survived the war intact, and until very recently retained the distinctive City character of relatively modest Victorian and Edwardian frontages conforming to a slightly meandering medieval alignment. Here, the coherence of the streetscape has been shattered by two ill-sited blocks: on the east side of Bishopsgate, facing Threadneedle Street with glaring orange–yellow reflecting glass is a 'slickist' speculative work; south of it is the much more carefully executed and much slicker Banque Belge by Gollins, Melvin and Ward. The installation of this modernist ensemble, two buildings which manage to relate neither to each other nor to anything around them, required the removal of a civilized row of buildings including Norman Shaw's only remaining work in the City, Baring's Bank of 1881, which was never listed despite repeated requests and protests by the Victorian Society. The wide setback of the new blocks conforms to the City's plan for widening the whole length of Bishopsgate to accommodate the increased traffic which the City's planners hope will be attracted by the lavish width of their new London Bridge. The plan envisages the eventual lopping-off of Leadenhall Market's main entrance in Gracechurch Street and the demolition of Leadenhall Buildings at the southeast corner of Leadenhall Street and Bishopsgate. From our vantage-point a twenty-four-storey Brutalist bunker looms above it.

The splendid curved façade of John Gibson's National Provincial (now National Westminster) Bank, 1865, with a two-storey colonnade of fluted Composite demi-columns leads us north into Bishopsgate. Planning permission has been granted for a second Nat West Tower behind Gibson's façade, retaining the banking hall. The tower will be larger than Centre Point in Tottenham Court Road (see page 114). We cross Bishopsgate and proceed north past Second Empire classic and Baroque façades which stand in the way of the City's road planners. Opposite the massive base of Seifert's tallest block we turn under the archway leading to Great St Helen's, a refreshing green enclave with **St Helen's, Bishopsgate**, a survivor of the Great Fire, on the east side. This fourteenth-century church with its unusual double nave, once served both Benedictine nuns and parishioners. St Helen's, particularly noteworthy for its medieval and Elizabethan effigies, has been called 'the Westminster Abbey of the City'. St Helen's gigantic steel and grey glass neighbour to the south is the Commercial Union Building by Gollins, Melvin and Ward, 1969, built on a site previously interwoven with alleyways and courts like Great St Helen's.

Having survived the turbulent downdraughts of the Commercial Union's gusty piazza we ascend the steps to Leadenhall Street. To the east is the sixteenth-century **St Andrew Undershaft** which also survived the Fire. The tower's pinnacles are Victorian. To the west Wren's green copper dome and spire at St Peter's, Cornhill, and Hawksmoor's tall Gothic pinnacles at St Michael's, Cornhill, form a skyline ensemble. We turn south from Leadenhall Street into Whittington Avenue, leading to Horace Jones' **Leadenhall Market** of 1881. The market, with a flat dome above the crossing and glass-roofed timber arches over the wings, provisions City workers and Livery Company banqueters. Cast-iron City griffins crouch with folded wings above wreathed Doric capitals at the crossing.

We follow the curves of Lime Street south to Fenchurch Street. The prominent corner building to the west, nos. 39–40 Lombard Street, is a sombre and original eclectic palazzo of 1868 by the Francis Brothers. Their façade, bearing motifs from four centuries of Italian architecture, topped by a full-blooded cornice and balustrade, has recently been gutted. We cross it into Philpot Lane which has two small early eighteenth-century clusters on the west side: nos. 2–3, stuccoed and much altered, and nos. 7–8 Philpot Lane/no. 4 Brabant Court, with segmental heads, heavy sashes, and Doric door-case with a segmental pediment and fluted pilasters.

At the bottom of Philpot Lane we turn east into **Eastcheap**. A Victorian group contains two of the City's most exotic designs – no. 23, 1862, at the corner, Italian–Byzantine with stucco below and polychromatic brick above, brick-rusticated round arches and an intriguing cornice with heads of hunting dogs and wild boar above floral plaques – a reference to the 'Boar's Head' tavern, frequented by Falstaff, which stood here; and R.L. Roumieu's phantasmagoric twin-gabled Gothic work, no. 33 of 1868. The fanciful character of these buildings seems well suited to express their original use as warehouses for imported spices, wine and vinegar.

The view from the Monument to St Paul's. On the left, partially blocking Wren's silhouette, is the Cannon Street Station office building by J.G.L. Poulson. In the foreground is 80 Cannon Street under construction

Further east in Fenchurch Street, no. 43, stuccoed in the nineteenth century, with a timber Corinthian front at ground level, joins onto the south face of Wren's **St Margaret Pattens** of 1687 in Rood Lane, creating an entrance forecourt to the church. St Margaret's strong high polygonal leaded spire retains its dominance despite postwar encroachments. Great Tower Street to the east frames a view to the spire of the restored pre-Fire All Hallows-by-the-Tower. Beyond it are the turrets of the Tower of London.

We turn south toward Wren's parish church of **St Mary-at-Hill**, down an ancient and once intimately-scaled lane descending to the river, now torn open by uncoordinated development on the east side. An impressive clock projecting on a bracket identifies the church. The interior, with a dome on four pendentives, is Wren's most exquisite. Further south is the Watermen's Hall, stone faced with a Venetian window. The adjacent brick hall of 1786 appears to be in a state of disrepair. Next to St Mary a pediment bearing a skull and cross-bones marks the entrance to Church Cloisters, a narrow passage leading to **Lovat Lane**, a part of the Saxon Street network which is remarkable for its descending S-curve and for the retained homogeneity of its frontages. Lovat Lane lay fallow for some years, since the authorities refused to grant the Office Development Permits which would allow the conversion of its small commercial properties. At the same time the officials granted themselves and their bureaucratic colleagues permission for massive total clearance office redevelopment projects elsewhere. Private re-furbishment for small offices has finally been allowed here. Botolph Alley facing St Mary's west front gives a further impression of the intimacy which once characterized much of the City. The lanes and alleys do not meet the planners' daylighting codes, but City workers as well as visitors feel a strong attachment to these areas.

We emerge from Lovat Lane at the intersection of Monument and Lower Thames Streets, facing Horace Jones' **Billingsgate Fish Market**, with dolphins flanking Britannia on the pediment. To the east is the long brick neo-classic back façade of the Custom House; to the west is a large triangular cleared site awaiting redevelopment, and beyond is the Portland stone tower of Wren's **St Magnus the Martyr**, 1687, surmounted by an arched octagon lantern rising to a leaded ribbed dome and a spirelet on a small open-work tower. Rearing up behind is Adelaide House of 1924 at the approach to London Bridge. The barrel vault of St Magnus' spacious nave is intersected by large round clerestory windows, and is borne on giant order fluted Ionic columns. **The Monument** of 1677 by Wren and Robert Hooke rises north of St Magnus. Plaques and a relief sculpture by Cibber at the base, flanked by City griffins, commemorate the Great Fire; above is a giant fluted Roman Doric column supporting a viewing platform and a stone cylinder bearing a gilded fiery orb. The vista from the top rewards the climber with St Paul's dome in the full grandeur of its harmonic proportion.

As we move north along Fish Street Hill toward Eastcheap and Gracechurch Street, a glance back shows the Monument and St Magnus' steeple in impressive perspective array. **Cannon Street** to the west frames a long, angled vista to St Paul's south-west tower, marked by its clock faces. Beyond rises the Post Office Tower near Euston Road. Cannon Street was a short medieval alignment extended west in the 1840s by the City Engineer, J.B. Bunning, along the route of the main Roman thoroughfare to Ludgate which Wren echoed in his post-Fire Baroque townplan. The importance of the Cannon Street approach to St Paul's has yet to attract the attention of the City's and the GLC's planners.

On the north side of Cannon Street to the west are pleasant nineteenth- and early twentieth-century façades, some in the gabled red-brick and terracotta style rarely found in the City; others are Portland stone classic or Baroque. The harsh red polished granite facing of Cannon Street House, 1976, on the south, may have been intended as a reference to the Victorian red-brick façades nearby.

Abchurch Lane leads to Wren's **St Mary Abchurch**, completed in 1687. The church's south façade faces Abchurch Yard, an arresting triangular courtyard paved with circles of granite setts and lines of slate slabs. The body of the church is a simple red-brick box with quoins and round, round-headed and segmental-arched windows on the south side. Above rises a

The visually important triangular site bounded by Monument Street, Lower Thames Street and Pudding Lane was occupied by Victorian buildings of modest height which were demolished to make way for an awkwardly placed ten-storey office block, as yet unbuilt. In granting planning permission for this scheme, the Guildhall planning committee seems to have disregarded its effect upon views to the Monument and St Magnus Martyr

The view from Monument Street across the site of an approved ten-storey block to St Magnus Martyr and the Monument. Unprotected view

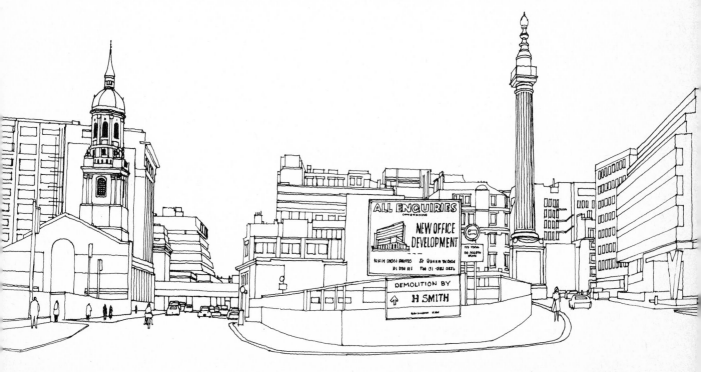

The approved scheme for demolishing a large part of the Bow Lane Conservation Area and replacing it with slick office blocks will affect views of St Paul's along Cannon Street

The Victorian blocks to be demolished in Cannon Street form an important part of the foreground to St Paul's

square brick tower, then an open lantern, an ogee lead dome and a spire. The adjacent buildings face the courtyard with façades in various shades of red, reflecting the warm tones of Wren's brickwork. St Mary's domed interior is surprisingly spacious, and recalls Wren's fascination with the transition from square to circle by means of an octagon, also shown at St Stephen Walbrook and in a compromise form at St Paul's.

We return to Cannon Street and are faced with no. 80 on the south, by Arup Associates, completed in 1977. The design, a black, totally opaque rectangular prism enclosed and partially supported by a diagonal net of stainless-steel tubes filled with water as a fire precaution, is surely the *reductio ad absurdum* of technological fetishism. Beneath the black box's underbelly is a sunken garden. The trees have died. Opposite Cannon Street Station is no. 103, a well-considered four-storey Italian–Byzantine design of 1886. Dwarfing it is a ballooning 'slickist' effort, Granite House, nos. 97–101. The designers of this inflated block seem to have taken literally the planners' jargon phrase 'building envelope'.

Before turning south into Dowgate Hill, we again note the vista west to St Paul's and the importance of the foreground Victorian block in Cannon Street; its delicate web of stonework seen in foreshortening blends harmoniously with the rhythms of the cathedral behind it. On the west side of Dowgate Hill and in College Street are Livery Company Halls – the **Skinners' Hall** has a neo-classic stucco façade of 1790 with a rusticated base and two-storey pilasters bearing Coade Stone Ionic capitals of the Bedford Square variety, with a pediment above; next is **Dyers' Hall**, a design of 1839 in red brick and stone which mixes the pedimented windows and quoins of the rising palazzo style with the Grecian pilasters and pediment of declining neo-classicism, perhaps out of deference to its neighbour on the north. West in College Street is the much-altered seventeenth-century **Innholders' Hall** with a scroll-pedimented eighteenth-century door-case and a swirling crest above it.

The view west from College Street presents two Wren steeples as contrasting variations on a theme. **St Michael Paternoster Royal** of 1694 rises in diminishing rings of columns and arches, bearing projecting entablatures and urns, to a round spirelet; beyond it **St James Garlickhythe** of 1717 ascends in square tiers with diagonally projecting paired columns and pilasters supporting square crockets and pinnacles. South of St Michael's is the City's recently installed Whittington Garden. North of the church in College Hill nos. 21–2 have two 'spectacular late seventeenth-century stone gateways' (Pevsner), which led to the college founded by London's famous fifteenth-century Lord Mayor, Dick Whittington.

Proceeding west along College Street we cross Queen Street, laid out by Wren on the axis of the Guildhall, and enter Skinner's Lane, leading to St James Garlickhythe. The interior is Wren's highest, and has been skilfully restored after bomb damage. Garlick Hill leads north through an area once associated with the spice trade toward Bow Lane. From St James's onward the alignment frames a view to the steeple of St Mary-le-Bow. The two lanes are interrupted by the scissors intersection of Cannon Street and Queen Victoria Street, but remain unique in having kept, until now, their intimate proportions and variety of small frontages. At the intersection the tall Gothic pinnacles of **St Mary Aldermary's** tower of 1704 come into view. On the east is the triangular Albert Buildings of 1871, with a fascinating variety of Italian Gothic rhythms. The new triangular block facing Albert Buildings on the west has attempted to mirror its townscape effect in modernist terms with questionable success.

Bow Lane lies to the north and framing its entrance on the west is the mid-Victorian Bath stone frontage which plans a key role as a foreground to vistas of St Paul's from Cannon Street to the east. This modest but effective design will almost certainly be demolished as part of an approved scheme to clear and redevelop a large part of the Bow Lane Conservation Area. The

'Skinners' Arms' pub at the corner and the small frontages in Bow Lane north to Watling Street will also disappear. The original proposal by the Skinners' Company for wholesale clearance and redevelopment of the block west of Bow Lane, which includes several listed buildings, was rejected by the City Corporation following spirited opposition by the Victorian Society. A slightly less ambitious scheme retaining some listed façades and an interior in Watling Street was also strongly rejected by the society and others as being totally unsuited to the character of the area, but received the quiet assent of the Guildhall in March 1977. Some months later, when the scheme became known, a City worker expressed his feelings about the Guildhall's 'conservation' policies in a letter to the *Evening Standard*: 'So many acts of Corporation delinquency have been condoned by us who work in and love the City, or what's left of it. We now surely realize that we need our City heritage. The authorities if they wished could help us retain it by encouraging and assisting in the retention of our old buildings, perhaps even providing incentives for tenants to remain. They have done exactly the opposite.' A new plan submitted to the City by a consortium of major insurance companies calling for further clearance of shops, restaurants and services in Bow Lane to the north and in adjacent **Well Court** has provoked several thousand objections.

We proceed past condemned buildings on the west side of Bow Lane, including the listed eighteenth-century **Salter's Court**, and past St Mary Aldermary's tiny churchyard on the east to **Watling Street**. Turning west we are presented with one of the City's most magnificent views – Wren's great dome fills the intimate space of the street. Most of the façades in Watling Street will be retained, including the interesting mixed stone and cast-iron front of nos. 24–6, but Watling Court to the south, an enclave of Victorian solidity and dignity on a small scale, will disappear. We cross Bread Street and then New Change, passing the neo-Georgian Bank of England extension, and Wren's tower of **St Augustine-with-St Faith**, and return to **St Paul's** Churchyard along the south side of the choir.

The south transept like the north has a semi-circular Corinthian portico. On the pediment above the cornice is Cibber's large relief sculpture of a phoenix rising. When laying out the new cathedral's position on the site of Old St Paul's ruins Wren asked a workman to bring him a stone to mark an important point. According to Wren's own account the workman handed him a fragment from a headstone bearing the single Latin word: RESURGAM – I shall rise again.

The Dean's Door is at the base of the south-west tower, dedicated to the Archangel Michael, Guardian of the Holy City, and to his successor St George, patron saint of England. Flanking the door and above it are William Kempster's volutes, garlands and cherubs. Kempster has sculptured the complex geometry of the volutes with musical fluency, and his exquisite carving of the three small winged cherubs beneath the pediment has infused the cold stone with radiance.

London's Future

MOST OF THE LONDON which fascinates visitors and inspires the affection of residents is comprised of remnants of the Georgian, Victorian and Edwardian periods, and of rare seventeenth-century and medieval traces. Modern additions are more or less tolerated as long as they remain unobtrusive, but are hardly a source of enthusiasm, although their designers confidently assure us that when their works have acquired the patina of time, they will be as dearly loved by our descendants, as Georgian terraces are by us.

The centres of the historic amalgam in the City and the West End have undergone a degree of change since the Second World War matched only by cities much more heavily damaged in that conflict, and by North American cities shattered by the onslaught of Urban Renewal. Less than five percent of Central London was destroyed in the Blitz; by 1965 the office space lost in the war had been replaced five times over. Most Londoners would agree that recent changes have been for the worse, both architecturally and socially. Throughout the heart of London over-scaled, anonymous, single-use development, approved and often instigated by 'the world's most sophisticated planning mechanism' has repeatedly crushed the delicate scale and eradicated the intricate variety so essential to London's unique ambience. The irreplaceable remnants of London's traditional urban fabric, in some places still holding together in coherent patches, in others sadly torn and scattered, are still vital, functioning parts of a living city and will remain so only as long as Londoners remain vigilant.

The Débâcle

After the Second World War dire warnings were issued by the architectural and planning professions that unless London were both thinned out and rebuilt 'comprehensively' upwards, the city would choke from overcrowding. Mr Robert Mellish, Labour MP for Southwark and Bermondsey, explained in Parliament that when he was a junior housing minister in 1964, 'I was advised that at all costs London must be denuded of population and industry because it was growing too fat. Foolishly enough I believed that and took the advice of these great planners. I spent my time doing all I could to urge people and industry to leave London. I look back now and realize that was the worst advice any government has been given.' The central government adopted its experts' strategies, while at local authority level townplanners armed with powers of compulsory purchase and the mechanisms of comprehensive redevelopment often joined forces with private speculators fixated upon high rent office space in order to realize their vision of large road interchanges punctuated by gleaming towers. Centre Point, standing empty for twelve years above half of an uncompleted roundabout is perhaps the best-known symbol of London's Age of Planning.

After two decades of such activities large parts of inner London lay derelict. Londoners 'voted with their feet' against the city of tomorrow built for them: 100,000 have left yearly for the last decade. 500,000 manufacturing jobs, one-quarter of London's industrial employment, have been lost since 1970. 9000 acres of land lie vacant in inner London: 55% of it is in local authority hands, 25% more is owned by statutory bodies, 100,000 homes are boarded up, more than half belong to local authorities, and 21 million square

feet of offices lie vacant. How much of this desolation is a direct result of the planners' intervention, and how much has been due to what they call 'complex social and economic forces over which London's planners have no control' is a matter of heated debate, but it seems obvious that 'changes in transport technology and in the bank rate' do not fully explain London's urban malaise.

Writing in February 1977 to *The Times* in defence of his profession's achievements, the president of the Royal Town Planning Institute announced that 'the ordinary layman is still impressed by the fact that 40 per cent of all housing has been built in the last 30 years; that the worst slums have been visibly eradicated from our great cities.' But *The Times*' television critic Michael Church expressed a prevailing attitude when he wrote: 'If there is one thing on which all Londoners would now agree, it is that the architects and planners who occupied positions of municipal power in the 60's should be put in the stocks, and that when all the available rotten eggs have been thrown they should be made to live out the rest of their miserable lives in the concrete hells they have created.'

Considering the extent of the débâcle for which they are now both generally held responsible it is not surprising that the professions of

Centre Point, vacant since its completion in 1965, its 'piazza' shunned by pedestrians, is the symbol of London's Age of Planning. In the foreground are Cambridge Circus and 84 Charing Cross Road. Planners seem invariably to draw the boundaries of Conservation Areas down the middle of streets, as if they were dealing with postal zones or statistical areas. The blinkered approach of GLC and Camden planners has led them to exclude visually important buildings in Cambridge Circus and Shaftesbury Avenue from the Seven Dials Conservation Area just across the street, leaving the Circus open to speculative excess; 84 Charing Cross Road and its neighbours will be replaced by a large-scale office scheme once the developers, Town and City Properties, have sufficiently 'convalesced' from the property débâcle of 1973

architecture and townplanning each disclaim their own role in it and loudly defame their former partners in the 'urban design team'. The spectacle they present is distinctly unedifying. Architects maintain on the one hand that, as prisoners of parsimonious clients, they have no more control over their designs than their own plumbing sub-contractors; on the other hand they are robbed of their creative freedom by the planners. It would be naive to suggest that these architects might draw strength from the examples of sacrifice and achievement set by Wren, Nash, Pugin and Street, since, as Sir John Summerson has pointed out, the fundamental principle of modernism, transcending all stylistic factionalism, lies in 'obedience to the programme'.

The prevailing attitude of architects towards the planners who have the statutory obligation of reviewing their designs was clearly stated at the 1977 annual conference of the Royal Institute of British Architects by Mr Michael Manson who asserted that 'to require an experienced architect to submit his design to a local authority for approval was like telling David Hockney or Graham Sutherland to submit to a hanging committee of house painters'. His colleagues responded with enthusiasm to his further assertion that 'if Hampton Court, St Paul's, or Carlton House Terrace were to be built now they would without doubt be rejected as out of keeping with their surroundings'.

At the 1976 summer conference of the Royal Town Planning Institute, the Architects' Journal reported that 'loud laughter was the response of 700 planning officers on hearing the Royal Institute of British Architects' demand for all architect designed buildings to be free from aesthetic control'. The distinguished architect Mr Roy Worskett, planning officer for the City of Bath announced to the assembled planners that he 'now totally despaired of architects' ability to fit new buildings into the historic street scene'.

In view of the conflict between those responsible for guiding London's future physical form it seems in order to review the relative merits of their claims. Townplanners are disposed by training and inclination to 'paint the urban canvas with a broad brush'. Since the collapse of the property boom and the advent of strong conservationist pressure they find their duties mostly confined to the detailed examination of architects' small-scale schemes, and the resulting professional friction is understandable. Planning officers are employed by local authorities to advise the elected representatives of the council in their decisions. While good advice is sometimes ignored, planners seem generally to prefer telling councillors what they would like to hear, particularly during times of economic stringency and staff cuts.

Planners lack formal visual training, and although some display sound visual judgment, all are compelled to review buildings according to categories developed by the theorists of modernism and set out in DOE circulars – 'height', 'bulk', 'material' and 'verticality' and 'horizontality'. These descriptions suffice for, and indeed exhaust, most modernist works, but are somewhat less than adequate to deal with the subtleties of historical architecture. According to the planners' guidelines, buildings of the eighteenth century are 'horizontal', those of the nineteenth 'vertical'. The Victorian buildings surrounding Trafalgar Square are thus 'vertical', those in the vicinity of Somerset House 'horizontal'. The attempt to civilize works of modernist hardliners by subjecting them to these rigid categories seems doomed to failure.

While design control imposed by planners seems destined to produce, at best, mediocrity, the vast majority of architects seem incapable of designing sympathetically in an historical environment. They look upon the old urban fabric from across a great abyss: as relics from a bygone era, perhaps inspiring sentimental admiration, but based on principles and displaying features of no relevance to their own problems and purposes. Obedience to the Zeitgeist forbids architects from using past works as a source of inspiration, or indeed education. The modernists' historical ideology

Detail of the façade of G.G. Scott's St Pancras Station Hotel. The qualities of historical architecture elude the planners' rigid categories - 'vertical, horizontal', etc. - simplistic formulae that are the DOE's guide to architectural taste

continues to cripple both the members of the older generation, for whom reified space, flowing in, around and under buildings remains the essence of architectural expression, and the younger architects who see their task as 'cultural communication' to be achieved by 'manipulating signs' drawn from the modern movement's own bleak history.

Brutalism's weighty collapse brought down the modernists' theoretical framework. In its place the avant garde, or more accurately, the rear guard of modernism has put up a gimcrack edifice composed of spare parts drawn from the grab-bag of structural linguistics and stuck together with the old Zeitgeistian glue. The judgments issuing forth from this peculiar contraption, once stripped of their jaw-breaking jargon, are often commonplace and sometimes remarkable. Alvin Boyarsky, head of the Architectural Association School, has announced that the contemporary city is an 'archaeological junk heap'. This seems an accurate description of those parts put up in the last thirty years, but hardly does justice to the civilized urban pattern evolved during the eighteenth and nineteenth centuries.

The present state of the architectural profession's aesthetic ideology and the evidence provided by recent buildings in London strongly suggest that freeing architects from design restrictions would have genuinely horrifying results. Yet the level of mediocrity resulting from the system of planners' control, and the long delays associated with it have reached an intolerable level.

There are possible ways out of the dilemma. One suggestion offered has been the appointment of an 'aesthetic Czar' who along with a small staff would assume full personal responsibility for the evaluation of designs, subject to the statutory assent of the councillors of the GLC. The system has its precedent in the old position of Surveyor-General occupied by men of the stature of Christopher Wren and William Chambers. The 'Czar's' position would resemble that of the *Senatsbaudirektor* in West Berlin, occupied by prominent architects in private practice for periods of up to three years. The advantage of the proposal, that it centralizes and pinpoints responsibility, is also its greatest drawback. Assuming that an architect, or perhaps an art historian, of sufficient stature and judgment would accept such a post, he would be tied to the cumbersome mechanism of the GLC, far removed from local tastes and attitudes, and would be able to deal adequately with only a small proportion of London's building applications, leaving the rest to the old system or to chance.

The system of local citizens' design review boards, or community panels, has operated successfully abroad, particularly in the United States.

Volunteer members of local amenity societies, residents' and businessmen's associations and the local chapter of the RIBA, after technical briefing by planning officers would make their recommendations to councillors' planning committees who would be expected, though not compelled to accept them. Unlike the planners, the design review boards would represent a variety of the community's tastes and interests, and unlike the politicians' planning committees, the review boards composed mainly of concerned laymen could be expected to bring a genuine interest and dedication to their task. Controversy would no doubt arise, and review boards' heated debates, held in public, might generate the sparks needed to stimulate the designer. Architects submitting their schemes would be required to illustrate them in their context. In cases of major applications and of projects affecting Conservation Areas, site visits by the review board and by the planning committee would be mandatory.

A similar proposal was included in the report of a planners' working group published in November 1976 calling for the abolition of the system of Structure Plans set up by the Town and Country Planning Act, 1968, and its replacement by decentralized control and a new openness in public affairs. The 1968 act was irrelevant, and according to the *Architects' Journal's* precis 'trying to plan and nurture the development of living communities through our statutory process of plan-making and review is as doomed to failure as Leonardo's attempts to design a flying machine.'

The Erosion of London

While controversy about the function of planning and the role of architects continues, the destruction of London's urban character, and of its architectural heritage goes on, not dramatically as in the days of wholesale clearance, but quietly, bit by bit. In areas like Soho and Covent Garden well-organized and articulate community groups have brought large-scale physical damage to a standstill and now devote their efforts to preventing detrimental changes of use. In the case of Covent Garden speculative office schemes are being attracted by the sound and adaptable physical fabric and the congenial ambience which the Covent Garden Community Association, struggling for homes and workshops, saved from the GLC planners. Also saved was the Garden's extraordinarily varied mixture of craft and light industrial workshops, of specialized commercial services, and residential enclaves. GLC officials seem to have been embarrassed by the Council's ten years of planning which froze improvement, drove out one-third of the area's residential population, and left gaping demolition sites at its centre. The Council's planners, under the watchful eye of the Community Association, now require, in accordance with Conservation Area legislation, that every application for change of use within the Garden's Conservation Areas be signposted by notices three feet high, informing passers-by of the intention to convert a scullery kitchen to a glass-blowing workshop, and of their right to object. These elaborate safeguards have not been applied to Trentishoe Mansions, vandalized by the GLC as a prelude to its replacement by 200,000 square feet of speculative offices, since its key site at Cambridge Circus lies just outside the Seven Dials Conservation Area.

The Soho Conservation Area, lying just across Charing Cross Road from Covent Garden is under the jurisdiction of Westminster Council. Since the Piccadilly Circus scheme collapsed in 1973, Soho has been spared the intervention of planners and their grand schemes, and in fact the area has suffered more from the planners' absence than from their presence. The 1976 annual report of the Soho Society which represents the area's two thousand residents pointed out that 'Soho remains an area under stress. Exploitation, neglect, and indecision have all added dangers. A constant reduction in low cost housing stock, illegal change of use, and the increase in business rents continue to force out of the area the legitimate businesses and craftsmen traditional to Soho.' The illegal take-over of properties in the Conservation

Covent Garden's rich mixture of specialized services, crafts and light industrial activities will continue to inspire the area's regeneration if the illegal change of use to offices can be controlled

Area by sex shops and massage parlours poses the most serious problem and is met by the Council and its planners with indifference. The *Soho Clarion* remarked in February 1977 that 'Until Westminster City Council takes its powers of enforcement of the planning law seriously, the long-term conservation of the area must remain in doubt.' As a result of residents' pressure, the GLC finally began a well-publicized campaign to limit those activities over which it had licensing powers.

In peripheral areas, or in parts of London where communities are less well organized and articulate, or where they do not exist, the planning bureaucracies left to themselves seem invarably to follow the path of least resistance, sometimes also followed by those bodies with a statutory obligation to protect buildings and areas of architectural and historic value. Cases of small- and sometimes not so small-scale dereliction and destruction are numerous. Whole rows of good Georgian houses were pulled down in Ebury Street, near Victoria Station, in 1976. The officially designated 'Outstanding Conservation Area' at Spitalfields in the Borough of Tower Hamlets has seen over the last decade the destruction of a dozen listed early eighteenth-century houses of architectural distinction and of particular historic value for their connection with the Huguenot silk-weaving trade. In September 1977 members of the Spitalfields Trust, a housing charity dedicated to preserving and rehabilitating the remaining houses, after frantic appeals to the GLC and Tower Hamlets proved futile, occupied houses themselves in order to ward off demolition which, though legally authorized, was felt to be wholly unjustified. Their intervention saved the houses.

The 1977 annual report of the Victorian Society listed sixteen cases of important historical buildings in London under threat or in urgent need of official attention. Among the most serious were warehouses at St Katharine Dock opposite the Tower of London. 'B' Warehouse of 1825 by Philip Hardwick is a Doric colonnade listed building of sombre grandeur. Requesting permission to demolish, the developers Taylor Woodrow submitted to the GLC in September 1976 that 'rotted, partly burnt, bomb damaged, incapable of beneficial use, ''B'' Warehouse, like a brontosaurus, is a creature of a by-gone age.' In an earlier submission requesting permission to demolish 'C' Warehouse nearby, Taylor Woodrow maintained that it detracted 'from the dignity of Hardwick's grand conception', and marred 'the splendour of ''B'' Warehouse'. Granted permission to demolish 'C', Taylor Woodrow then turned on 'B'; it was not only a 'brontosaurus' – it was of 'no particular architectural or engineering importance'. The Department of the Environment, upon whom the decision rests, appears likely to agree.

The City

The City of London presents the most extreme case of an area with an architectural heritage of national, and indeed of world importance which lacks the defences provided by a strong community of well-organized residents. The Barbican scheme was an ambitious attempt to extend the City's residential base, and most of its 5000 residents live there. A recent survey showed that only about a third of the Barbican's tenants were full-time residents, and their Association points out that the City's decision to let part of the housing to companies' nominees has sounded the death-knell for the original concept which was to recreate a community in the City.

The property market's characteristic cycle of boom and bust, paralleled and in fact augmented by the alternating application and relaxation of central government controls on office building, found its most uninhibited expression in the City in the activities of the asset strippers and dubious property companies which flourished there in the 1960s. The normal process of destruction and replacement which characterizes all urban growth took on an aspect of fevered excess. Even after the devastating collapse of the property market in 1973, the City continued on its course of demolitions, 'like a dying animal biting its wounds'.

Although the City's finance still seems tied to property speculation and specifically to the development of City offices, with major pension funds and insurance companies developing large office blocks there, the City is also the centre of a great variety of other activities – ship brokerage, commodity transactions, insurance, and foreign exchange – and its success and world pre-eminence in these fields depends not upon the size of its office blocks but on the 'delicate web of understandings', the close relations between those expert in these markets, their physical proximity and the nexus of specialist firms supporting them. The form of the Victorian and Edwardian City, adapted and refurbished, would seem well suited to these activities, which are the real generators of the City's 'invisible earnings', but in 1962 the Guildhall decided that London's historic core should take on the aspect of a classic American 'downtown', with a high-rise cluster near the Royal Exchange, and the Royal Fine Arts Commission agreed. In response to aesthetic criticism of their City of Tomorrow, the Guildhall invariably waves the flag, insisting that the environmental quality of a boom-town in the Klondike is a necessary feature in the City's struggle to maintain its place in face of foreign competition. A visit to Zurich would show that the Swiss have been able to maintain an efficient and extremely healthy world centre of banking and foreign exchange in the heart of the medieval city without constructing a single high-rise block.

High-rise London

In 1957, the year the London County Council approved the Shell Building, the Royal Fine Arts Commission warned that approval of the proposed Hilton Hotel in Park Lane would set the precedent for ruining the pastoral character of London's parks. Following the Commission's advice, the LCC refused the application, but its decision was reversed at ministerial level following an appeal by the owner. Until 1956 London's skyline had been controlled by the London Building Act of 1888, which limited building heights to the width of the street or to a maximum of eighty feet plus a two-storey roof, with an allowance for 'architectural features'. The regulations stemmed from Queen Victoria's displeasure at seeing the towering mass of Queen Anne's Mansions, a formidable atrocity 151 feet high, which rose above the gardens of Buckingham Palace. At the same time in Chicago the first steel-framed buildings were rising above the notoriously unstable Chicago mud. It was not, as technological critics claim, the subsiding London clay which prevented high buildings here, it was the Building Act of 1888 and the consensus which supported it. Sixty-eight years later the restrictions were removed, and the LCC announced it would consider cases 'on individual merits'. In 1962 the LCC defined its five principles of evaluation: density, availability of transport, function, wind and aesthetics. The following year the London Government Act granted the LCC, later the GLC, its 'strategic prerogative' to review all applications for buildings in excess of 150 feet in central London and 125 feet elsewhere. Since its inception in 1965, the GLC has reviewed applications for 2893 high buildings; of that number 451 applications were subsequently withdrawn, 353 were refused, and 2089 were approved.

In May 1968 the Ronan Point tower in East London collapsed. In 1970 the GLC High Building Policy was published as part of the proposed Greater London Development Plan. The policy included a map indicating areas 'sensitive' to high buildings and designated views to be protected from high-rise intrusions. They were: Buckingham Palace from the Mall, Kensington Palace from Kensington Gardens, St Paul's from Westminster Pier, Chelsea Hospital from the Embankment; and the skylines of the Royal Parks and the principal London squares. The same year the GLC approved the 600-foot-high Nat West Tower in the City.

The 1973 report of the Leyfield Panel which had reviewed the GLDP urged that the High Building Policy diagram be given the force of a statutory map.

The City's planners still think that their sparse and virtually inaccessible upper level walkways are the way to deal with pedestrians. A traffic interchange has left Wren's charming red-brick St Benet's haplessly stranded. Inigo Jones is buried there

In 1976 the revised GLDP was approved by the Secretary of State for the Environment. The High Building Policy was presented in the form of an 'Urban Landscape Diagram', not as a statutory map. Areas were classified, as 'sensitive' or 'inappropriate' for high buildings, rather than as 'permitted' or 'forbidden'. Six famous views in Central London were to be protected as in the 1970 plan. The criteria which high building proposals would be expected to meet were that they would not mar the skyline or intrude to the detriment of a famous or pleasant view, that they would be carefully related to their surroundings, and would be of 'outstanding architectural quality'.

Two days after the topping out ceremony of the Nat West Tower in the City, Mr Patrick Cormack, Conservative MP for Staffordshire South West and secretary of the all-party Parliamentary Heritage Group, introduced a Private Member's Bill in Parliament calling 'for the protection of skylines of historical interest or outstanding natural beauty', throughout Britain. Local authorities were to be obliged to designate views to be protected and include them in their structure plans, with the Secretary of State retaining reserve powers of designation. The basic intent of the legislation was to adapt the GLC's well-meaning but ineffectual policy of height control and view protection and give it statutory force. In presenting the bill, Mr Cormack pointed out that in West Berlin the *Landes Konservator* had the power of veto over any building which affected the skyline or visual field of the monuments under his protection, and that in Switzerland a federal regulation required the erection of a scaffold marking the outline of any proposed building, no matter how high, before planning permission was granted. The first reading of the bill was accepted without opposition. On the same day the president of the French Republic issued an edict forbidding structures in excess of seven storeys throughout France.

Reporting the reaction of prominent planners to the Skyline Bill, *The Guardian* stated that 'there is a considerable weight of professional opinion which believes the whole business superfluous'. At the bill's second reading in Parliament in May 1977 Mr Guy Barnett, Under Secretary for the

The City has granted planning permission for a twelve-storey office block at New Fresh Wharf which will obscure this famous view of St Paul's, as well as views from Tower Bridge.
Unprotected view

Environment, expressed the view of the Department's planners when he disputed the necessity of new legislation and maintained that the present review in terms of 'bulk, height, materials and vertical and horizontal emphasis' offered adequate protection. He added that it was extremely difficult to legislate anything as nebulous as aesthetic taste. In reply Mr Cormack noted that nowhere in the present planning law or in the DOE's circulars was any mention made of 'skyline' or of 'views', and that existing review procedures seemed to be patently inadequate in view of the literally thousands of fine vistas which have been disfigured over the last decade. He reminded Mr Barnett that the precedent for legislating taste was well established in British planning law, and referred him to the listing and Conservation Area legislation. Although the bill was forwarded to committee without opposition, this vitally needed legislation will not become law until the government chooses to support it.

Some commentators have maintained that we have seen the last of high buildings in London. There seems little desire at the moment to continue with this uneconomic and unpopular form of construction, but it should be

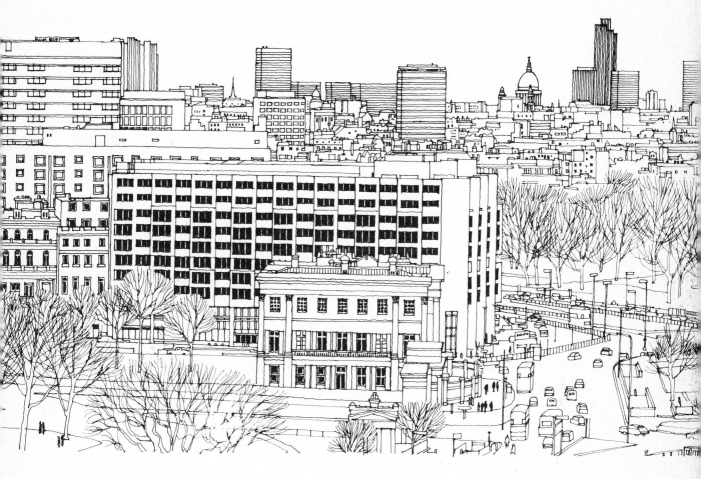

View from the Park Tower Hotel across Hyde Park to the Hilton, which 'set the precedent for ruining the pastoral quality of London's parks'

pointed out that in the City of London, where questions of economy or popularity bear little weight, there remain fifty-five sites designated as appropriate for high-rise construction, in addition to the nineteen tower blocks which now stand there.

Preservation, Conservation, and View Protection

There are some 29,000 listed buildings in London, and while this may be a reassuring statistic, it may also be seen as a reflection of the magnitude of the threat to London's architectural heritage. The same could be said for the Conservative legislation which provides London's areas of townscape value with more stringent protection than in comparable European cities. The Civic Amenities Act of 1967 which gave legal status to the concept of Conservation Areas may be seen as the defensive counterpart to the provisions of the Town and Country Planning Act, 1947, which provided the legal framework under which developers were encouraged to undertake vast projects in partnership with local authorities in areas where previously only piecemeal development had been possible.

The translation of the principles of conservation to larger urban settings resulted in the proposals for skyline and view protection which themselves reflect the devastation caused by a decade of high-rise construction. One may argue that the London skyline is already ruined, and while this is certainly true of the large-scale vistas such as those of the City from the Thames, or from the hills of north London, there remain a good many urban vistas of value which merit legal protection. Some of these were pointed out in the preceding series of townscape walks, many others lie outside the confines of the City and the West End. Most are street vistas, and many are of intimate scale. The GLC Urban Landscape Diagram and its schedule identified six views in Central London which deserved protection. The studies associated with this book have established about about sixty more, many of which are currently under threat. They often lie across, or outside Conservation Areas, and are sensitive to the intrusion of buildings considerably lower than the 150-foot limit above which the GLC would be able to exercise its 'strategic prerogative'. Since these views comprise some of the most important remaining parts of the neo-classic and particularly of the later Victorian and Edwardian townscape, their protection is now particularly vital. Listing procedures unfortunately are still heavily influenced by the notion that Victorian works are inferior to those of the Georgian and neo-classic periods, and the 'collapse of taste' in 1840 is more or less official dogma in the Department of the Environment. Buildings designed after that date stand a good chance of being ignored unless they manifest a technological advance, are the work of an important architect, or are considered an outstanding example of a style. The most intriguing and individual of the eclectic mixtures are thus the most likely to be excluded from the official lists. These works, with their rich skylines and 'impressionistic' detail are among London's most important buildings from the point of view of townscape. The authorization of listing on the basis of a building's position in a group was set out in the Town and Country Planning Act of 1944, but it remains the least used of that act's provisions. Since the greatest threat to London's townscape is now focused upon buildings of the post-1840 era the original instructions contained in the 1944 act should now be fully implemented.

The Civic Amenities Act requires local authorities to designate areas with qualities which should be 'preserved or enhanced'. There are a good many Conservation Areas which require more preservation than enhancement, and these are often defined as 'Outstanding Conservation Areas', which unfortunately offers them no more protection than areas with less strength or coherence. It would seem more logical to single out those areas of quality where architectural change should be discouraged and redesignate them as 'Preservation Areas', that is as essentially listed ensembles, while granting more freedom for 'enhancement' elsewhere. It should be emphasized once again that buildings which match their neighbours in 'bulk, height, material, verticality or horizontality' can hardly be counted on to enhance them, and that character of detail, scale, texture rhythm, proportion and skyline also need to be carefully observed, bearing in mind that intelligent contrast is often called for.

The Next Boom

The reaction against increased listing and expanded Conservation Areas has set in on several fronts. Not surprisingly, much of the opposition comes from architects and townplanners, many of whom condemn conservation as 'middle-class cosmetics', and worse, as 'blocking the upward social mobility of disadvantaged groups'. The only 'disadvantaged groups' whose upward social mobility seems to have been blocked by conservation are in fact the planners, architects and developers themselves. From other quarters, particularly in the City, demands have been made for a moratorium on new listings, while the DOE minister responsible for conservation, Lady Birk, announced in October 1976 that 'we shall not be giving as many marginal

In the spring of 1977 Camden Council began construction of London's last high-rise block of flats in Newton Street, Covent Garden. Camden has kept up its ritualized liaisons with the property speculator Mr Joe Levy. The most recent issue of this odd relationship has been the fourteen-storey council flats shown above, designed for the council by Col. Seifert and jammed onto a tiny site immediately behind Town Hall in High Holborn. Camden approved the design in November 1976

buildings the benefit of the doubt'. According to Dan Cruickshank in the *Architects' Journal*, 'marginal buildings' were precisely those to be listed for their contribution to the townscape. A view not unlike Lady Birk's was expressed by the chairperson of the GLC planning committee who announced in May 1977 that henceforth the Council would be less perfectionist, and would prefer to see 'bad buildings in place of dilapidated houses'. In July 1977 the president of the Royal Institute of British Architects led a delegation of his colleagues to 10 Downing Street where he pleaded for government measures to insure more work for architects. In October 1977 the DOE announced extensive cuts amongst its investigators which, it acknowledged, would lead to a marked slow-down in the listing of historic buildings. On 16 May 1977 the Secretary of State for the Environment, Mr Peter Shore, announced in Parliament the removal of Office Development Permits from all but the largest schemes. He further announced that several large speculative office schemes were about to be approved in inner London, and that this would aid the construction industry and 'ensure that the property market is geared for the eventual upturn in the economy'. In looking forward to that event it should be borne in mind that according to a report in *The Times* of October 1977, 'there are 625 projected redevelopment schemes in London involving sites of five acres or more', and that the Greater London Development Plan approved in 1976 lists forty-eight Comprehensive Redevelopment Areas 'where powers conferred for this purpose remain in force'. More immediate and more concrete is Camden Council's plan to build 300,000 square feet of speculative offices, the equivalent of three Centre Points, in Euston Road. Local residents have rightly called for a public inquiry.

Broad Street Station in the City . In 1868 The Builder *surveyed all the London rail termini and came to the conclusion that 'Broad Street Station is in its exterior superior to any other London station. In its air of lightness . . . it shows considerable taste.' The station is not listed and stands under serious threat of demolition for a BR office scheme.* Unprotected view *An impression of one of several alternative BR schemes for office blocks and a new station on the site of Liverpool Street and Broad Street Stations*

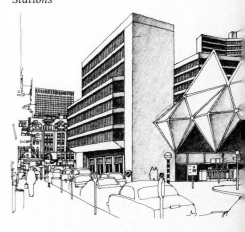

Planning by Inquiry

In cases where a local authority grants itself planning permission, or where it has demonstrated an obvious bias, the use of a public inquiry to investigate the issue seems warranted. The system of planning by inquiry applied to every major or controversial scheme, as it usually is, indicates the almost complete lack of public faith in the ability of local authority planning mechanisms to deal fairly and adequately with issues of any consequence. The system also implies either an enormous public trust in the sense of justice of the Secretary of State and his senior advisers in the Department of the Environment, or a confidence in the effectiveness of the public muscle-flexing now usually displayed at inquiries to sway the decision of the Secretary, who is after all a politician. Although public inquiries are called by the Secretary in order to inform himself of the views and evidence surrounding an issue, he is free to disregard an inquiry's findings if these conflict with government policy.

Despite this, and despite the great expense of time and effort involved, objectors generally prefer to place their trust in the Secretary's wisdom, and local authority planners and councillors are often glad to be relieved of the necessity of taking difficult or unpopular decisions. Objectors to planning schemes can find themselves liable for heavy legal expenses. Two young teachers who led the unsuccessful struggle against the GLC scheme to cover St Paul's Playing Field in Hammersmith with a housing estate had their sense of public responsibility rewarded by an order to pay £7000 costs. Sometimes inquiries provide the kind of fireworks and dramatic *coups de théâtre* which may partially explain their popularity. At the long and bitter Archway Road Inquiry in north London, the choruses of shouting, stamping and singing used by 'middle-class mobsters' to drown out Ministry of Transport testimony drove one ministry official to run amok and begin assaulting members of the public. Subsequently the objectors produced statistics which demonstrated that the Ministry of Transport's thirteen-year-old road-widening scheme had been based on 'utterly impossible' traffic forecasts. The DOE Inspector examined these statistics, closed the inquiry, and sent the scheme back to the ministry for its 'reappraisal'. In other cases, like the Cleveland Street Inquiry in Westminster the proceedings have been quietly depressing. Evidence prepared by the GLC Historic Buildings Division in defence of twenty threatened listed Georgian houses was withdrawn shortly before the inquiry began as a result of the change in GLC political leadership following the May 1977 elections. When a *samizdat* copy of this evidence obtained from dissidents at County Hall was read out at the inquiry, it was greeted by the DOE Inspector's ill-disguised boredom. Westminster planners, who asserted that the buildings, though structurally sound, should still be demolished since the owners 'had no intention of repairing them' admitted under cross-examination that in the seven years since they had declared the buildings a 'slum' they had never actually spoken or communicated with the owners (see also p. 37–8).

At the autumn 1976 Liverpool Street Station Inquiry some of the more obvious shortcomings not only of British Rail's scheme to demolish the station's listed western sheds, but also of the system of Planning by Inquiry, became glaringly obvious. British Rail's plans for a new station, and for 1.2 million square feet of offices next to and above it, provoked this response from Stephen Gardiner in *The Observer* of 16 January 1977: 'Of course, without the public inquiry system immense damage would be done to places of considerable architectural quality. Yet there are times when the plans under discussion seem so foolish one wonders how they could ever have come to be conceived at all – and, having been conceived, how they could have been allowed to get so far that an inquiry had to be called. The present inquiry at Guildhall into the Liverpool Street Station affair will, I suspect, be a case in point.'

John Chesshyre, who led the Liverpool Street Station Campaign (LISSCA)

to save the unlisted portions of the station as well as the Grade I western sheds described a situation often encountered by private objectors and amenity groups: 'One might expect the planning authority to obtain the railway engineering advice, instead of unpaid, spare-time, voluntary funded LISSCA. Indeed, the issue of who is spending public money on what is highlighted by BR's massive expenditure on legal representation (two QCs and a junior) and consultants (principally, Fitzroy Robinson, architects, and Nathaniel Lichfield, development economists), not to mention armies of its own staff committed to working on the case. LISSCA, whose case, also backed up by building economists and leading conservation architects, demonstrates alternative means of achieving both railway and development objectives at enormously reduced public cost, is very hard pressed to raise the money to pay its own lawyers, and may well have to withhold its expert witnesses from cross-examination because of the cost of keeping them at the inquiry. Where's the natural justice in that, and is this in the best interests of a full examination of the facts at the public inquiry for the benefit of the Secretary of State?'

The art of architecture and of city building has traditionally been involved not only with the realization of immediate aims and private purposes, but also with a sense of responsibility to the community as a whole, and to its history. In Nicholas Hawksmoor's words: 'Whatever is good in its kind ought to be preserved in respect to antiquity, as well as our present advantage, for destruction can be profitable to none but such as live by it.' This sense is still manifested by those who take it upon themselves to enter the often unequal struggles in the arenas of public inquiries. One feels that Hawksmoor would do the same.

As part of their programme of planned dereliction BR have refrained from painting Liverpool Street Station's cast-iron sheds for fourteen years. At the public inquiry BR's Counsel pointed to the station's 'dilapidated image' as a justification for demolition. The fees BR paid to its consultants and lawyers for their specious arguments could have protected the cast-iron cathedral with several coats of paint

Index